St Antony's Series

Series Editors

The St Antony's Series publishes studies of international affairs of contemporary interest to the scholarly community and a general yet informed readership. Contributors share a connection with St Antony's College, a world-renowned centre at the University of Oxford for research and teaching on global and regional issues. The series covers all parts of the world through both single-author monographs and edited volumes, and its titles come from a range of disciplines, including political science, history, and sociology. Over more than forty years, this partnership between St Antony's College and Palgrave Macmillan has produced about 400 publications. This series is indexed by Scopus.

Nicolás Zuluaga Afanador

The Sociological Legitimacy of the Special Jurisdiction for Peace of Colombia

palgrave
macmillan

Nicolás Zuluaga Afanador
Faculty of Law
Pontificia Universidad Javeriana
Bogotá, Colombia

ISSN 2633-5964 ISSN 2633-5972 (electronic)
St Antony's Series
ISBN 978-3-032-21911-4 ISBN 978-3-032-21912-1 (eBook)
https://doi.org/10.1007/978-3-032-21912-1

Cover credit: Matteo Legrenzi, 2023

This Palgrave Macmillan imprint is published by the registered company Springer Nature Switzerland AG
The registered company address is: Gewerbestrasse 11, 6330 Cham, Switzerland

To Colombia, may peace live within us

Acknowledgements I could not have navigated through this journey without the support of many incredible human beings. I would like to thank my mother, Sylvia, my brother, Federico, and my father, Jorge, for always listening, for encouraging me to pursue my aspirations with joy and trust, and for making me fell at home in every circumstance and every place.

I also wish to thank Alejandra Castañeda for her unwavering, support, love, and enthusiasm throughout these years and especially this project. Her encouragement and thoughtful feedback was invaluable in improving this book. She, along with Isabela Gutiérrez, Laura Valderrama, Laura Insignares, Cristina González, were always just a phone call away. Their stories, advice, and laughter warmed me even on the coldest, greyest days of winter. Thank you!

I am also grateful as well to all those who made my time in Oxford feel like a new home. Our shared meals, conversations, and plans illuminated my journey in many ways.

My thanks also go to the anonymous external reviewer, whose comments were most helpful to address recent develpoments in the field.

Last, but certainly not least, I am deeply grateful to Leigh for her guidance throughout this process. She helped me organise my ideas with innovative thinking, and her encouraging words and trust were an essential source of comfort as I wrote this book.

Competing Interests The author declares that he does not have any competing financial or non-financial interests in relation to the content of the book.

Ethics Approval The author declares that informed consent was obtained from individual participants.

About This Book

The Special Jurisdiction for Peace (JEP, for its acronym in Spanish) is the set of national judicial institutions in charge of adjudicating crimes committed by the FARC-EP and the Colombian Government during the internal armed conflict between 1964 and 2016. Since its inception, the JEP's legitimacy has been contested mainly because it was created as a key aspect of implementation of the 2016 Peace Agreement, which was narrowly rejected in a referendum.

However, several signs suggest that the JEP's legitimacy may be higher than initially expected. These include the difficulty of modifying the JEP's design, by-laws or operation; the institution's comparatively better reputation relative to older judicial institutions and the fact that most of the JEP's rulings are fulfilled.

This book endeavours to explain this legitimacy puzzle by verifying the extent to which the factors known affect judicial institutions' legitimacy—e.g. diffuse and specific support, salience, obedience and age— are consistent with the JEP's case. Drawing on polls, media studies and data collected in fieldwork (including numerous interviews and participant observation at hearings), it proposes specific variables that shape the legitimacy of transitional justice judicial institutions.

The book also identifies signs indicating whether these factors are contributing to the erosion or strengthening of legitimacy, and introduces a scale designed to assess the legitimacy of transitional justice tribunals.

Finally, it evaluates the JEP's legitimacy and outlines several contributions to the existing literature on judicial legitimacy in transitional contexts.

An epilogue examines the first two sentences issued against those most responsible for patterns of macro-criminality, specifically, the kidnapping of individuals by the former FARC-EP and extrajudicial killings perpetrated by Armed Forces agents. It also assesses the impact of these rulings on the JEP's legitimacy and on its future operation.

Contents

About the Author

Nicolás Zuluaga Afanador is a Colombian lawyer, having graduated from Pontificia Universidad Javeriana, Bogotá (2019). He holds an MPhil in Latin American Studies from the University of Oxford (2024) and, previously, worked for the Special Jurisdiction for Peace, first as a clerk and later as a researcher involved in opening one of the macro-cases. He also served a researcher for the University of Essex, studying the implementation of restorative sanctions and the possibility of collectively fulfilling the duty of providing reparations within the Special Jurisdiction for Peace. This work resulted in a coauthored paper, "Anticipated TOAR and Proper Sanctions: An Informed Reflection for the Special Jurisdiction for Peace", published by Dejusticia, a well-known Colombian think thank, as well as the working paper "The Collective Fulfilment of the Duty of Reparation in the Special Jurisdiction for Peace", published by the Essex Transitional Justice Network.

He currently works as a professor at Pontificia Universidad Javeriana and a law clerk at the Constitutional Court of Colombia, in Bogotá, Colombia.

List of Figures

List of Tables

CHAPTER 1

Introduction

Abstract The Introduction analyses the paradox Colombia has faced during most of its history. Compared to other Latin American nations, this country has relative stable democracy institutions—with periodical elections, and a relatively independent judicial branch—while it has endured several cycles of violence. Probably the most recent project to stop these has been the Peace Agreement signed in 2016 between the Government and the "Revolutionary Armed Forces of Colombia – People's Army". The JEP plays an essential role in this project, as it is the judicial institution in charge of holding accountable the members of the FARC-EP and the Colombian Armed Forces who committed serious human rights violations between 1964 and 2016, as well as those civilians and public servants that accepted the JEP's jurisdiction. Despite the importance of the JEP's mission, many sectors of the Colombian society have contested its legitimacy because they disagree with its origin, design and operation; and the critiques have been increasing. However, over time, the JEP has built some legitimacy capital among sectors of the civil society, the international community and the Colombian State. This book aims to explain how the JEP built its sociological legitimacy and what factors impact this process.

N. Zuluaga Afanador, *The Sociological Legitimacy of the Special Jurisdiction for Peace of Colombia*, St Antony's Series,
https://doi.org/10.1007/978-3-032-21912-1_1

Keywords Transitional justice · Special Jurisdiction for Peace · Colombia · Sociological legitimacy · Internal armed conflict · FARC-EP · Construction of legitimacy · JEP · Armed forces

Since the beginning of the twentieth century, Colombia has lived in a paradox. Compared to many countries of Latin America, Colombia has built a stronger and more stable democracy. Yet, at the same time, it has endured consistent cycles of violence that may be difficult to accept in a democracy. Probably the most recent significant project to stop these cycles of violence has been the Peace Agreement signed in 2016 between the Government and the "Revolutionary Armed Forces of Colombia – People's Army"[1] (FARC-EP, for its Spanish acronym), the most powerful guerrilla in Colombian history, with more than 13,000 combatants at the time of their demobilisation in 2017 (Truth Commission of Colombia 2022b, 566). The Special Jurisdiction for Peace (JEP, for its Spanish acronym[2]) plays an essential role in this project to curb violence. It is the judicial institution in charge of holding accountable the members of the FARC-EP and the Colombian Armed Forces who committed serious human rights violations between 1964 and 2016, as well as those civilians and public servants that accepted the JEP's jurisdiction.

Despite the importance of the JEP's mission, many sectors of the Colombian society have contested its legitimacy because they disagree with its origin, design and operation; and the critiques have been increasing. Over time, the JEP has built some legitimacy capital among sectors of the civil society, the international community and the Colombian State. What explains the JEP's legitimacy in the aftermath of an internal armed conflict that divided the Colombian society? What factors reinforce or erode the JEP's legitimacy? These are the matters this book will address, and the following sections will unpack them.

[1] In Spanish, "Fuerzas Armadas Revolucionarias de Colombia – Ejército del Pueblo". Throughout this book, many acronyms will keep their Spanish version, as they are more known in this form than in the English one.

[2] In Spanish, "Jurisdicción Especial para la Paz".

1.1 The Colombian Paradox: A Relative Stable Democracy Amid Cycles of Violence

Several facts show that Colombia has had a particular democracy compared to those of the region. Colombians have one of the oldest democracies in Latin America and the 24th oldest in the world (Desjardins 2019). In August 1886, they promulgated a constitution that lasted 104 years, until July 1991. Since 1910, elections have been held every four years, except for the only dictatorship in the twentieth century. Curiously, it lasted almost as long as the four-year presidential term, between 13 June 1953 and 10 May 1957, and its origin was tolerated by the two hegemonic parties, the Liberal and Conservative Parties, as a temporary solution for their violent disputes. Due to its lower levels of repression in relation to other dictatorships in Latin America, it is considered by some a *dictablanda* / "soft dictatorship" (Truth Commission of Colombia 2022b, 62).

Another sign of the strength of Colombian democracy is that the judicial branch has acted with relative independence from the Government and Congress, setting limits to them. Since 1957, when the dictatorship was over, the Supreme Court justices have been elected through the system of "co-optation", where the justices themselves elect their new colleagues. Although the Supreme Court of Justice depended on the Government for securing its funding and administrative operation until 1989, it consistently set limits to the President (Guevara 2011, 159–62). For example, during the 1970s and the 1980s, the Supreme Court struck down constitutional reforms and laws that limited the Court's power. These reforms were aimed at strengthening the executive branch: aligning the ordinary judicial processes with those of the military criminal jurisdiction (1976), increasing presidential control over the judiciary (1979), and reducing judicial autonomy by granting judicial powers to police authorities (1985). Decades later, in 2010, the Constitutional Court handed down the decision that has arguably tested its independence the most since its creation. This judicial authority, in charge of the judicial review of constitutional reforms after the 1991 Constitution, struck down Law 1354 of 2009, which called for a referendum on authorising a second re-election of arguably the most popular president in Colombian history, Álvaro Uribe Vélez (BBC News Mundo 2010). Over the course of his eight-year period, 72% of the population held a favourable opinion of him, on average (El Colombiano 2010).

Despite having an apparently democratic and stable regime, Colombia has simultaneously endured alarming, recurring cycles of violence, which successive peace agreements have attempted to end, often unsuccessfully. As Gutiérrez Sanín (2020), Melo (2021), and the Colombian Truth Commission (2022b) have skilfully documented, the country has experienced at least two cycles of violence since the twentieth century and, according to Gutiérrez Sanín, may be experiencing a third one. The first cycle, known as "La Violencia (The Violence)", was a "non-declared civil war" that spanned from the 1940s to the early 1960s, primarily involving conflict between the Liberal and Conservative parties. In the second period, "the counterinsurgency war" (1964–2016), the anti-governmental guerrillas, the Armed Forces and paramilitary groups participated in a complex war. The guerrillas aimed to overthrow the government militarily, while the Armed Forces defended the regime, often with the help of paramilitaries. The main cause of victimisation was not the armed confrontations, but rather direct or indirect attacks on civilians, who were accused by the various actors of collaborating with the enemy (Grupo de Memoria Histórica 2013). This cycle ended with the Peace Agreement between the Government and the FARC-EP. In its aftermath, the levels of violence decreased, kidnappings and massacres plummeted (Gutiérrez Sanín 2020, 18–20). Despite the benefits of the FARC-EP demobilisation, Colombia may be experiencing a third cycle of violence, in which the only guerrilla left, the National Liberation Army / "Ejército de Liberación Nacional" (ELN for its acronym in Spanish), FARC-EP dissidents, and successors of the paramilitary groups hold dominance over certain territories and compete to control illegal economies such as drug trafficking and illegal mining, while State Forces attempt to gain control over these historically neglected territories.

In the following sections, I will describe the two first cycles to provide historical context for the Peace Agreement. I then describe the negotiation and approval of the Peace Agreement, with a focus on the creation of the JEP. Finally, I explain the contested nature of the JEP's legitimacy.

1.1.1 The First Cycle of Violence: "La Violencia" (Late 1940s–1958)

While academics and intellectuals debate the exact beginning of it, there is consensus that the first major cycle of violence in the twentieth-century Colombia began in the late 1940s. In 1946, the Conservative leader Mariano Ospina Pérez won the elections against a divided Liberal Party that had held power since 1930. Although Ospina proposed to create a National Union, including Liberal politicians in his cabinet, his initiative ultimately failed.

Simultaneously, from 1947 onward, Conservative local leaders, often with the complicity of authorities, encouraged attacks on Liberals in order to reaffirm Conservative dominance locally dominance, especially in rural areas. Following a purge of all Liberal members from the police force, the Conservative Police—known as "Chulavita Police"[3]—along with illegal paramilitary units composed of police and army personnel, referred to as "Pájaros" or "Birds" perpetrated multiple atrocities, killing hundreds of Liberals. These violent acts were extreme: in some cases victims were dismembered, as documented by Ferry in his graphic account of Colombia's internal armed conflict (2012).

One illustrative example took place in 1949, when the Conservative Governor of Antioquia—one of Colombia's most economically developed departments—resigned because many of his fellow Party members incited the burning of several municipalities. A few days later, Rionegro, a Liberal stronghold in Antioquia, was burnt with the help of departmental government employees (Melo 2021, 216).

As a defensive reaction to the escalating violence across the territory, Liberals, especially peasants ("campesinos") took up arms to defend themselves, forming bandit groups ("bandoleros") or more organised Liberal guerrillas. These armed organisations were particularly powerful in the eastern plains of Colombia.

In February 1948, Jorge Eliécer Gaitán, then the Liberal Party's most popular leader, denounced these crimes during a silent march. More than 40,000 people gathered in silence at the political heart of Colombia, the "Plaza Bolívar" in Bogotá, where the Supreme Court's Palace of Justice, the Congress, the Presidential Palace and Bogotá's Cathedral—the most important church in Colombia—are located (Melo 2021, 214).

A little more than a month later, on April 9, Gaitán was abruptly murdered a few blocks away from the "Plaza Bolívar", while he was leaving his office, triggering an intense social unrest, known as "El Bogotazo". In Bogotá, numerous followers of Gaitán protested in the streets, sacked stores and burnt the headquarters of "El Siglo" (The

[3] It was called "Chulavita" because many of the members were recruited in the county Chulavita of the Soavita's municipality in Boyacá, a department of Colombia located in the Andes (Figueroa Cordero 2022, 4).

Century), the most famous conservative newspaper, and several government offices. Similar situations occurred in other big cities, such as Barranquilla, Cartagena and Medellín, and smaller municipalities, like Magangué and Corozal (Truth Commission of Colombia 2022b, 53). These events fuelled the existing conflict, which later became even more intense with the election of the radical Conservative, admirer of Francisco Franco's regime, Laureano Gómez (1950–1953).

Gómez's term was characterised by the political persecution of Liberals, an attempt to impose a constitutional reform with corporatist elements, and the escalation of violence, as Gomez was radicalising even against the will of some Conservative leaders. Supported by some members of both the Liberal and Conservative parties, Rojas Pinilla's dictatorship was intended to curb the violent disputes between these political organisations. In his first speech after seizing power in 1953, Rojas Pinilla proclaimed on the radio: "no more blood, no more depredations in the name of any political party. No more quarrels between the children of the same immortal nation" (Villar Borda 2020). In the following days, he signed an amnesty for all those involved in the conflict and created programmes to reintegrate former combatants. The Chulavita police and the "Pájaros" ceased to operate. Many Liberal guerrillas demobilised, yet some kept fighting.

Rojas' dictatorship ended in 1957 with the agreement of the "Frente Nacional" (National Front), formalised the following year. Supported by significant military sectors and businessmen, the political leaders of the Liberal and Conservative parties agreed to share power for 16 years (1958–1972) by alternating control of the Presidency every term and ensuring that each party had half of the members in every Corporation (Congress, Ministries and even the Supreme Court). The "Frente Nacional" effectively ended the violent political confrontation between the traditional parties. By the mid-1960s, some Liberal guerrilla groups were still operating, but the two parties were no longer involved in direct political violence (Gutiérrez Sanín 2020, 2–3). Contemporary estimates suggested that the conflict had resulted in over 200,000 deaths (Borda et al. 1962). However, a more recent study using econometric methods estimates that the number of politically-related deaths between 1949 and 1958 may be closer to 39,412 (Romero-Prieto and Meisel-Roca 2019).

1.1.2 *The Counterinsurgency War (1960s–2016)*

The period of peace following the National Front did not last long. The second cycle of violence, the "counterinsurgency war", began some years after the end of "La Violencia" (1960s) and lasted until 2016. During this period, inspired by the successful revolutions of Cuba, China, and the Soviet Union, several guerrilla groups emerged in the 1960s and the early 1970s and tried to seize power. Initially, the State confronted them timidly, but progressivelly it enhanced its military power, increased its attacks—despite being involved in human rights violations itself—and eventually signed peace agreements with most of the organised armed groups, including the paramilitaries.

Simultaneously, around 1977–78, landowners and local politicians created paramilitary groups to defend themselves from guerrilla operations. Over time, these armed groups became increasingly involved in the drug trafficking business and used their forces to terrorise rural populations for the benefit of certain local elites, among other atrocities. Especially between 1995 and 2001, many companies benefited from the purchase of land from peasants who had fled paramilitary violence. One notorious case is that of the Córdoba Livestock Fund, a cooperative of livestock producers that bought hundreds of hectares at below-market prices from displaced peasants in the Urabá region (Sánchez et al. 2018).

As stated above, in the 1960s and in the early 1970s, several guerrillas emerged in Colombia. Inspired by Marxism, communism, and the success of the Cuban revolution, these organised armed groups were founded as a reaction to the extreme concentration of land, inequality, the lack of State presence in rural areas and the notable closure of the political system due to the National Front. Having presence in different parts of the country and sometimes disputing the control over the territory, they all wanted to seize power. At the same time, some of them participated in the political system. For example, the FARC-EP that had a strong relationship with the Communist Party (Melo 2021; Truth Commission of Colombia 2022b).

The guerrilla groups' origin was varied. In 1964, a guerrilla following the Cuban example, the "Ejército de Liberación Nacional" / "National Liberation Army" (ELN for its acronym in Spanish) was created. Supported by the Colombian Communist Party, the FARC-EP was founded in May 1966 in the rural municipality of Marquetalia, after the Government had violently attacked its predecessor armed structure, almost to the point of extinction. In 1967, expelled and dissident members of the Colombian Communist Party organised a guerrilla inspired by the Chinese Revolution: the "Ejército Popular de Liberación" / Popular Army of Liberación (EPL in Spanish). In 1974, an urban guerrilla specialising in spectacular operations emerged: the "Movimiento 19 de Abril" (the 19th of April Movement, or M-19). The name came from the date on which the last elections of the National Front were held. The official candidate, the Conservative Misael Pastrana, won by a slight margin over the former dictator Rojas Pinilla, and many claimed that the election had been marred by fraud (Truth Commission of Colombia 2022b).

Between 1964 and 1974, the guerrilla groups did not represent a major threat to the Colombian State (Melo 2021; Truth Commission of Colombia 2022b). But from 1974 on, they used the illegal resources at hand more effectively. Businessmen and political leaders kidnapping increased, especially between 1978 and 1986. Frequently, the ELN extorted oil companies under the threat of blowing up pipelines. The FARC-EP charged a fee for the coca crops in their territories ("gramaje") and benefitted from the other stages of production.

At the end of the 1980s, the Government agreed to the demobilisation of the M-19 and most of the EPL guerrillas, along with a full amnesty for their members. The M-19 created the "Alianza Democrática" ("Democratic Alliance"), a party that became one of the leading forces of the Constitutional Assembly that promulgated the current Constitution in 1991. Meanwhile, the FARC-EP and the ELN had conversations with the Government, but did not sign any Peace Agreement. One of the few measures that emerged from these peace negotiations was the creation of the Unión Patriótica in 1985, a party founded by the FARC-EP and the Communist Party. However, at least 4,616 of its members were killed in the following years (JEP Government Board 2024), constituting a "political genocide", according to the Truth Commission (2022b, 213–18).

The 1991 Constitution did not bring the expected results in terms of peace. In the 1990s, the main remaining guerrilla groups, the ELN and the FARC-EP, strengthened their military power and extended their control over the territory. As a result, by the end of the 1990s and early 2000s, according to the JEP, the FARC-EP had become a serious threat to the Colombian State (*Auto 019 de 2021* 2021). It had taken over several municipalities, among them Mitú, the capital of the Vaupés Department (1998). It had also implemented a policy to kidnap rich citizens, and used this practice to restrict the freedom of thousands of innocent people in order to raise funds to finance the war. Several politicians were kidnapped, among them, Ingrid Betancourt, a Presidential Candidate (2002), and 12 members of the Assembly of the Valle del Cauca Department (2002), one of the richest departments of Colombia. Colombians were afraid to use roads, because there were occasional guerrilla checkpoints to kidnap travellers. This was called "Pescas milagrosas" ("Miraculous fishing"), as guerrilleros expected to find someone wealthy among the many families driving along the road. In total, according to the JEP, between 1992 and 2012, the FARC-EP kidnapped 21.396 people (*Auto 019 de 2021* 2021).

The most intense years of the "counterinsurgency war" were between 1996 and 2002. The guerrilla groups strengthened their military power, the paramilitary groups united under the name of "Autodefensas Unidas de Colombia" ("United Self-Defense Forces of Colombia", AUC in Spanish) and increased their military operations, the Colombian State lived an economic and institutional crisis, while the drug trafficking business fuelled the conflict (Grupo de Memoria Histórica 2013, 33). After Álvaro Uribe Vélez came into office, a new era started. Under his government, the AUC demobilised. Between 2004 and 2006, 30,944 men and women laid down their arms. Apart from the success in reaching an agreement with the AUC, the guerrilla groups' military power was severely reduced. The enhanced Armed Forces attacked aggressively the FARC-EP, killing some of its top commanders "Raul Reyes" (2008), "Mono Jojoy" (2010), Iván Ríos (2010) and Alfonso Cano (2011) (Red + Noticias 2023). Furthermore, the Armed Forces conducted several successful rescue operations, among them the "Operación Jaque" ("Operation Checkmate"), where Ingrid Betancourt was liberated (2008).

This cycle of violence ended definitively in 2016, when the Government and the FARC-EP, the most powerful guerrilla in Colombian history, signed a Peace Agreement. The atrocities that the civil society was forced to endure were ruthless. After integrating 112 databases, the Special Jurisdiction for Peace, the Truth Commission and the Human Rights Data Analysis Group estimated that, in the context of the internal armed conflict, 450,664 people lost their lives (1985–2018); 121,178 were forcedly disappeared (1985–2016); and 50,770 were kidnapped (1990–2018) (Truth Commission of Colombia 2022a). Adjudicating all these crimes is not an easy task. That is why the discussions about creating an integral transitional justice system took longer than other points of the negotiations' agenda.

1.1.3 Peace Negotiations (2010–2016)

Peace negotiations with the FARC-EP started shortly after Juan Manuel Santos won the 2010 election as Uribe Vélez's chosen succesor, following the Constitutional Court ruling that had prevented Uribe from running for a third term. After an exploratory secret phase (2010–12), the negotiations between the FARC-EP and the Government were held in Havana, Cuba, between 18 October 2012 and 24 August 2016, when the parties reached the first Final Peace Agreement (FPA). According to Jorge Orlando Melo (2021, 287), the talks succeded largely because they were motivated by a desire to reduce the damage of a long conflict involving a weakened FARC-EP. By contrast, the previous negotiations (1999–2002) had attempted to put an end to a conflict with a guerrilla group with increasing military power.

Building on the lessons of previous, unsuccessful peace processes with vague agendas, this process' framework was clearly delimited. It consisted of six general points, each accompanied by specific subtopics: (1) a policy for integral rural development; (2) political participation; (3) the end of the conflict, including mechanisms for demobilisation and reintegration; (4) a solution to the problem of illicit drugs; (5) victims, with a focus on measures for compensating those affected by the internal armed conflict; an (6) implementation, verification, and approval of the FPA (National Government of Colombia and FARC-EP 2012).

Although the conversations took almost 4 years, the progress was relatively constant until the discussion of the fifth point—the creation of the Integral System for Peace, an integral transitional justice system designed to guarantee the victims' rights. After several forums and conferences that facilitated the participation of civil society, scholars and victims, the parties reached agreements on the first point (May 15, 2013), on the second point (November 6, 2013) and on the fourth point (May 12, 2014) (Biblioteca Abierta del Proceso de Paz colombiano 2021).

The negotiation of the fifth point was more complex and time-consuming than the others. Throughout 2014, the FARC-EP and the National Government mandated the United Nations and the National University of Colombia to organise forums for fostering the victims' participation. These events were held in Villavicencio, Barrancabermeja, Barranquilla, and Cali—municipalities representing different regions of Colombia. Furthermore, five victims' delegations travelled to Havana to present their perspectives directly to the parties. On August 22 2014, the parties installed a Commission of 12 experts and 2 rapporteurs to analyse the: (1) the origins and causes of the internal armed conflict; (2) the factors and conditions that have contributed to the persistence of this armed confrontation; and (3) is most notorious effects and impacts on the population.

The experts produced diverse analyses, showing that there were disagreements on these subjects, but many converged in highlighting certain "geological flaws" in the construction of the Colombian State, as the rapporteur Eduardo Pizarro Leongómez noted. These underlying issues, depending on the circumstances and actors involved, were partly the foundations of the outbreak of violence. Examples include: land concentration, institutional weakness, deep income inequality, a persistence combination of armed struggle with legal political participation; and the precarious—and in some cases, traumatic—presence of the State in many areas of Colombia (Leongómez 2015, 6). The report responded to the Parties' agreed objective to present a multiplicity of perspectives rather than a single vision. The report did not contain an official or a single truth; on the contrary, it constituted an input to a democratic and pluralistic dialogue about the origins of the conflict (Leongómez 2015, 4–5).

1.2 The Creation of the JEP

According to Juan Manuel Santos, President at the time of the peace negotiations, the discussion about the victims' point took longer than expected—from May 7, 2014, when the parties signed a statement about the principles of the discussion, until the end of 2015. What is more, it was "the longest and most important of the process" (2019, 381) and brought the process to the brink of the abyss, particularly due to the difficulty in reaching an agreement on the justice system (Santos 2019, 369).

The parties swiftly consented on the creation of an extrajudicial Truth Commission that would: explain the origins, facts and consequences of the internal armed conflict; identify those responsible of the conflict-related atrocities, recognise the victims' rights; and, chiefly, provide recommendations for guaranteeing the non-repetition of the crimes. Furthermore, the peace delegations also designed the Special Unit for the Search for Persons deemed as missing, a humanitarian mechanism specifically in charge of looking for those missing in the context of the internal armed conflict. Yet, by June 2015, they were stuck in the terms of the judicial system that would adjudicate the crimes committed during the war.

On the one hand, the society expected the FARC-EP to pay for their crimes in jail. Humberto de la Calle, chief negotiator for the National Government, explains it boldly: "Since the beginning of the conversations, in the polls more than 75% demanded prison for the guerrilla" (De la Calle Lombana 2019, 98).

On the other hand, that same society had the urge of building the peace. But the FARC-EP was seeking the broadest amnesty possible, insisting that their members should not face imprisonment for their crimes. They argued that their leaders needed to remain free so they could lay the foundations of a new political party after the signing of the peace agreement.

In his book about the peace process, President Santos boiled down these ideas to the following sentences: "no subversive group signs the peace to go to prison. Neither in Colombia nor anywhere else in the world" (2019, 378–79). In his opinion, the final goal of every negotiation with a guerrilla group is replacing the armed struggle with political engagement (Santos 2019, 385). As was frequently stated during the peace process, this meant "changing bullets for votes".

Therefore, both parties' negotiators had the difficult task of finding the middle ground between the thirst of justice and the desire for peace. Apart from the abovementioned tensions, this was a difficult task because, in the last decades, Colombia had assumed international obligations to investigate, adjudicate and sanction international crimes, especially serious human rights violations and war crimes.

In June 2002, the Congress ratified the Statue of Rome, which obligated the States to effectively prosecute war crimes and crimes against humanity. The treaty also established the International Criminal Court (ICC) to intervene in cases where national jurisdictions failed to comply with international obligations. Two months later, the Colombian President deposited a declaration to defer the treaty's entry of force until 2009, intending to preserve an opportunity to negotiate with guerrilla groups on more favourable terms.

By 2015, that window of opportunity had effectively closed. What is more, in 2013, the ICC's Prosecutor at the time, Fatou Bensouda, stated that there were sufficient grounds to conclude that crimes against humanity and war crimes under the potential ICC jurisdiction had been committed in Colombia. As a result, the country had to effectively fulfil its duty of prosecuting these crimes to avoid the ICC's action (De la Calle Lombana 2019, 102, 113).

Moreover, the Inter-American Court of Human Rights had also consistently established the States' duty of investigating, prosecuting and sanctioning serious human rights violations. However, in a 2012 decision (El Mozote and its surroundings vs. El Salvador), the concurrent vote of the judge Diego García Sayan argued that, in internal armed conflict contexts, such a duty was not absolute, and should be weighed against the duty and obligation to achieve peace (Interamerican Court of Human Rights 2012).

In practice, the use of amnesties for pardoning crimes—which the FARC-EP negotiators were referring to—was substantially limited to political crimes. Following the ICC and the Inter-American Court of Human Rights jurisprudence, crimes against humanity, serious human rights violations and war crimes could not be the object of amnesties whatsoever.

However, the States could determine their own sanctions, which could mean that the sanctions could be different from prison. The National Government proposed at least some time of imprisonment, whereas the FARC-EP suggested only restorative sanctions with no time in jail. The complexity of designing a judicial system that fulfilled international obligations and, at the same time, the National Government's and the FARC-EP's requests explained why there was not a substantial progress after one year of conversations on this topic.

Following the advice of an international advisor, the British Jonathan Powell, President Santos proposed to the FARC-EP the idea of creating an autonomous special commission of six jurist to discuss this subject (three appointed by each of the parties). The FARC-EP agreed, and the commission was created on July, 26, 2015. In two months, the Commission drafted the foundations of what is now known as the JEP.

The system was designed under some premises that were shared by all the jurists of the commission and were published the day after it was installed (Santos 2019, 385; Justice Subcommission of the 2016 Colombian Peace Agreement 2015). First, the objectives of the judicial system were mainly two: ensuring legal certainty for those who participated in the armed conflict (facilitating peace consolidation) and guaranteeing the satisfaction of the four victims' rights: truth, reparation, justice and non-repetition of the violent facts (Bermúdez Liévano 2018, 212). Second, the main legal frameworks of reference would be international human rights law and international humanitarian law. Third, following the Article 6.5 of the Protocol II to the Geneva Conventions, the Government would "grant the broadest possible amnesty to persons who have participated in the armed conflict". Yet, there were some crimes that could not be amnestied or pardoned; for example, the crimes against humanity and those defined by the Statue of Rome. Four, granting an amnesty, pardon or any legal benefit would not exempt those responsible of a crime from the duty of contributing to the truth. Furthermore, the extent to which a person provides truth determines the degree of their potential benefits. Five, whenever the amnesty or pardon does not proceed, the perpetrators will be sanctioned. Six, the mechanisms and proceedings for FARC members, State agents and other actors who may have participated in the internal armed conflict could be different but, at the same time, they should be balanced and equitable. Seven, the imposition of any sanction would not prevent the participation in politics.

Since this moment, three points were difficult to address (Santos 2019, 385–91). The first one was the sanctions imposed to the crimes that could not be amnestied or pardoned. In the beginning, the FARC was not willing to admit more than restorative sanctions without any restriction or deprivation of liberty. Conversely, the sanctions proposed by the Government included some time of prison. At the end, the parties arrived to a Solomonic measure: those who contributed to truth and acknowledge responsibility would receive sanctions, consisting of restorative actions and some restriction of liberty, which could not be imprisonment. Otherwise, they would receive prison sentences, if they do not contribute to truth or if they do so late in the process.

The second controversial point was offering the possibility of participating in politics to those who had committed serious human rights violations. Despite resistance from different sectors of society, this concession made sense in that the ultimate goal of a negotiation with a guerrilla was to turn in weapons to participate in politics. The FARC-EP delegation would not sign an agreement that would put them in jail or condemn them to ostracism in the political arena.

Lastly, giving equal treatment to members of the Armed Forces and guerrilla members was widely criticised, since in theory the first were acting to protect Colombian citizens. Although this may have seemed unfair to many Colombians, the Government argued that this measure would prevent the unfair standards of previous peace processes, where guerrillas were amnestied or pardoned and military personnel was prosecuted, held responsible and imprisoned.

Beyond the criticism, the JEP was a very important precedent for the world. This was the first successful attempt to create a national transitional justice system to fulfil the international duty to investigate, prosecute and sanction crimes described in the Statue of Rome. Until then, only Uganda had tried something similar in the midst of peace negotiations, but it had failed (Bermúdez Liévano 2018, 218). That is why in his visit to Colombia in 2020, the Deputy Prosecutor of the International Criminal Court (ICC) at that moment, James Stewart, stated that Colombia was a pioneer and example for the world in terms of designing a model that aims to investigate and prosecute those most responsible of crimes committed in the context of an internal armed conflict. In his opinion, the JEP could effectively sanction crimes that might be under the ICC's jurisdiction (Canal Institucional de Colombia 2020).

Moreover, it was the first time that the political reincorporation of former combatants happened while they were being held accountable for the crimes they had possibly committed (Bermúdez Liévano 2018, 244). In former President Santos' words: "I am certain that what we agreed on the issue of justice is the greatest and most innovative contribution of the Colombian peace process to peace in the world, because its principles and its development can be used as a model for unresolved conflicts"[4] (2019, 391).

According to Bermúdez Liévano (2018, 206, 270–79), the FARC-EP and the National Government were aware that the Peace Agreement, and especially the JEP, needed both legal legitimacy, complying the national and international legal standards, and social legitimacy in regard of the Colombian society. As the National Government delegation pointed out to the FARC-EP: "if we do not succeed in satisfying these two values

[4] Quote in Spanish: "Tengo la certeza de que lo acordado en el tema de la justicia es el mayor y más novedoso aporte del proceso de paz colombiano a la paz del mundo, pues sus principios y su desarrollo pueden servir como modelo a muchos conflictos aún sin resolver".

(legal and social legitimacy), the agreement will not have legitimacy. And without legitimacy, it will not be sustainable over time"[5] (Bermúdez Liévano 2018, 206).

Despite international praise and its innovative design, the JEP's legitimacy has been contested from its inception to the present day.

1.3 The JEP's Contested Legitimacy

Since the JEP's origin, former President Álvaro Uribe Vélez, well-known senator Paloma Valencia and their right-wing party *Centro Democrático* (CD) have represented the critiques of many sectors of the Colombian society against the Peace tribunal. As Andrei Gómez-Suárez notes, Uribe and the CD deployed the motto Peace without impunity / "Paz sin impunidad" as an emotional mechanism to elicit anger and unfairness. They claimed that any acceptable peace agreement must exclude impunity for serious crimes, and the JEP failed short of this standard.

In their opinion, the JEP was not an acceptable mechanism to bring about justice. The JEP was tailored to the FARC-EP's needs and fostered impunity in that allowed perpetrators of grave human rights violations to take office as congressmen while they should be in jail. What is more, instead of imprisoning terrorists that were responsible for the many of the most atrocious crimes in Colombian history, the JEP would favour the dialogue between victims and perpetrators and reparations that went beyond monetary means and entailed restorative actions that were not proportional to the committed crimes, like the construction of roads or reforestation. On the contrary, fair measures like the perpetrators' imprisonment would be used only for the cases of least cooperation.

Furthermore, the JEP unfairly equated crimes committed by Armed Forces agents to those committed by FARC-EP "terrorists", as the first only acted following their duty to defend the Colombian State and population (Infobae 2021, 2024).

In short, in Uribe and his party's view, the JEP was tailor-made to acquit the FARC-EP and seek revenge by incarcerating policemen, soldiers and civilians, imposing minimal and disproportional sanctions

[5] Quote in Spanish: "Si no logramos satisfacer estos dos valores, el acuerdo no tendrá legitimidad. Y sin legitimidad, no tendrá sostenibilidad en el tiempo», le dijo el equipo del Gobierno a las Farc."

compared to the war crimes that occurred during the internal armed conflict.

These critiques were not minor and had an effect on the Peace Agreement's approval. On August 24, 2016, the government and the FARC-EP announced that they had reached a peace agreement, after four years of negotiations. It would be submitted to a referendum on October 2 so the people could decide whether they approved or rejected the terms of the negotiation. This measure followed Santos' belief that popular vote was the best way of approving the agreement. He had in mind the successful voting of the Good Friday Agreement, which on May 22, 1998, was approved by 71% of the voters in Northern Ireland and 94% of voters in Ireland. On that occasion popular vote legitimised the Agreement, despite political differences.

In Colombia, former President Álvaro Uribe and the CD were the main campaigners against the peace treaty. As the manager of the NO campaign recognised, their goal was that people left their homes to vote out of anger ("apelamos a la indignación, queríamos que la gente saliera a votar berraca—de mal genio—") (El Espectador 2020). To do so, they consistently conveyed the emotional mechanism of "paz sin impunidad". As a result, a slight majority of 50.21% rejected the Peace Agreement and, hence, the JEP.

Once the results were announced, hundreds of citizens gathered across the country to express their support for the peace process. Every week, hundreds mobilised to pressure the parties and the NO campaign to renegotiate and find an alternative solution.

In this context, President Santos declared the renegotiation of the Agreement for some weeks (BBC News Mundo 2016b), and the JEP was a central point of discussion. Although most of the changes proposed by the negotiators of the NO were adopted, the parties of the Agreement refused to accept the imprisonment of the individuals most responsible for human rights violations and the ban on the FARC members from having seats in Congress (El País 2016).

Dissatisfied, Uribe Vélez and the CD did not support the approval of the Peace Agreement in Congress and they have been consistently opposing the JEP's operation. They frequently argue that the Peace Agreement was rejected in the Plebiscite; therefore, the JEP is illegitimate.

Finally, the Government and the FARC-EP signed a new version of the Peace Agreement in November 26, 2016, in the Teatro Colón in Bogotá. This version was approved by a vast majority in Congress, which during 2017 approved the constitutional amendments to put the Peace Agreement into place, among them the creation of the JEP on April 4, 2017 (BBC News Mundo 2016a).

Although the Peace Agreement was ultimately ratified, the CD has become one of the biggest parties in Colombia in recent decades. Just after the signature of the Peace Agreement, CD became the ruling party between 2018 and 2022: one of its members, Iván Duque, one of the NO campaign leaders, came into power as President for the same term, as the CD became the largest party in Congress. Moreover, though his popularity has been decreasing, former President Álvaro Uribe Vélez is still a popular public figure in Colombia. This would suggest that the opposition to the JEP has continued to thrive despite the change in governments, since Santos' administration.

Since 2024, the JEP has been challenged by a new set of actors who previously supported it: the FARC-EP itself and some members of the National Government delegation. The first have claimed that the JEP has been going astray from their original design, it has not granted as many amnesties as it is obliged to by international law, and it has used more of a retributive approach than restorative. They even implied that the judicial insecurity that the former combatants have been facing has forced some of them to reintegrate into illegal armed groups, and that they might ignore the JEP's rulings were the JEP to continue this course of action.

The second have claimed that the JEP has been investigating and prosecuting more individuals than it was designed for, taking longer than expected to fulfil its objectives. For example, Yesid Reyes, Minister of Justice during the negotiation of the fifth point, unsuccessfully sued the JEP's investigation strategy before the Constitutional Court, claiming that it was unconstitutional (El Espectador 2024). Similarly, in early 2025, Humberto de la Calle, leader of the National Government delegation for the Peace conversations, and Sergio Jaramillo, High Commissioner during the Peace conversations, argued before the Constitutional Court that the JEP was prosecuting those who were not the most responsible for grave human rights violations. In their opinion, this operation is unconstitutional because it breaches the constitutional selection principle of the JEP (Mauricio Villamil 2025).

Despite all this contention from the CD and the FARC-EP, it seems that the JEP has substantial legitimacy. As I will thoroughly describe in the following chapters, after many attempts at reform, the JEP structure remains unchanged and in the last year its personnel has increased. In fact, when it was necessary, many sectors of society and individuals mobilised to support the JEP's operation and structure.

Moreover, the JEP has taken many contentious decisions which have been complied by all the interested State institutions; most of the indicted FARC-EP and Armed Forces combatants have acknowledged their responsibility and have cooperated in providing truth and reparation, even in public hearings.

Further, some symbols of the JEP have been adopted by social movements. For example, on February 18, 2021, the JEP estimated that 6,402, innocent people were killed by the Armed Forces to be presented as casualties, commonly known as *falsos positivos* or false positives. Since then, this number has been frequently used by MAFAPO ("Madres de Falsos Positivos") to ask for the prosecution of the "most responsible" for ordering *falsos positivos* operations.

Following a series of hearings held by the JEP, during which former members of the Armed Forces acknowledged their responsibility in the *falsos positivos* scandal, many public figures could no longer deny the existence of these atrocious crimes. Even former President Álvaro Uribe Vélez—who had consistently rejected the occurrence of these crimes during his administration, and also their systematic nature—was compelled to admit their existence.

Additionally, the UN Security Council, the Prosecutor of the ICC and international organisations, like the European Union, have permanently supported the JEP. Lastly, the JEP is one of the judicial institutions in Colombia, arguably even of the State itself, with the most favourable image and in which most people trust.

The ambivalence nature of the JEP—marked by both contested legitimacy and broad national and international support—prompted the central research question of this book: What explains the JEP's legitimacy? Within this question, there are a set of concepts that require further clarification. I do so in the conceptual framework chapter. What follows is a discussion of the academic and empirical importance of the question.

1.4 Relevance of the Topic

Studying the JEP's legitimacy is important to the transitional justice studies because it is arguably the most recent and complete national mechanism to fulfil two demands that are apparently contradictory. States have the international obligation of investigating, adjudicating and sanctioning grave human violations, especially those who ratified the Statue of Rome. Yet, at the same time, States facing armed conflicts have the obligation to pursue peace. As a result, transitional justice designs must comply with international obligations and, simultaneously, offer enough legal incentives to make a potential demobilisation or regime change feasible. That is why, Karim Khan, the current Prosecutor of the ICC has referred to the JEP as "a model for the world" (International Criminal Court 2021). In that regard, this book tests the JEP as a model, contributing to better understanding how this mechanism may face challenges to its legitimacy. This study also focuses on how these obstacles could be overcome or, on the contrary, how they could worsen.

1.4.1 Testing the Success of the "Balanced Justice" Approach

Another reason for analysing the JEP's legitimacy is to understand if a "balanced justice" approach works, in that it effectively impacts the societal perception of justice and institutional trust, which, in turn, strengthens a democratic process of transition. In 2010, Tricia Olsen, Leigh Payne and Andrew Reiter published one of the first books that studied a large number of transitional justice mechanisms. In this document, they recommended the use of a transitional justice approach that until then had not been largely implemented and would improve the efficacy in "strengthening democracy and reducing human rights violations" (2010). They called it a "balance justice" approach.

After using quantitative methods to analyse transitional justice in 161 countries between 1970 and 2007, they created a database including 848 transitional justice mechanisms of five different types—trials, amnesties, truth commissions, reparations and lustration politics. Then, they studied their impact on strengthening democracy and reducing human rights violations, contrasting variables such as the Freedom House Index for democracy and the Physical Integrity Rights Index for human rights.

The authors noted several conclusions that further the existing knowledge on transitional justice. Unlike contemporary literature, they claimed that economic and political constraints did not necessarily prevent countries from implementing transitional justice. Rather, the success of that transitional justice hinged on particular choices that protected it from political and economic constraints. In their opinion, the best design was a "balanced approach", in that "combining and sequencing mechanisms can provide that protection [from economic and political vulnerabilities] and lead to success on democracy and human rights goals" (Olsen et al. 2010, 6). According to their data, the most successful transitional justice systems included trials and amnesties and adding truth commissions would also improve success. This finding challenged existing transitional justice literature, which advocated for particular mechanisms.

Following the maximalists claims, trials "are essential to accountability for human rights violations and to building democratic institutions" (Olsen et al. 2010, 154). Yet, States cannot put everyone on trial. If countries attempted so, they would use legal and financial resources that cannot be used to implement other projects, which could increase the State's legitimacy and further democracy.

An alternative is to reduce the number of trials for key perpetrators and provide amnesty to the others, while allocating more funds to institutions in charge of protecting human rights and democracy. As a compliment, truth commissions are helpful to clarify some of the truth that does not emerge in trials, compensating the fact that not every perpetrator is prosecuted. These extrajudicial mechanisms are also spaces where restorative justice could take place, where victims and perpetrators could start dialogues with each other. In a few words, the authors argued that transitional justice systems should take into account that "a balance exists among legal imperatives, public safety, and pragmatic considerations" (Olsen et al. 2010, 154).

The JEP is the materialisation of the "balanced justice" approach. It is part of the Integral System for Peace, a "holistic" system created by the Peace Agreement with the FARC-EP that combines all the different transitional justice mechanisms studied by Olsen, Payne and Reiter, except from lustration policies: a truth commission, reparation policies, trials and amnesties (in the JEP). The system even includes a new mechanism: a Unity for the search of people deemed as missing, who are more than 126,000 people, according to its estimates (2025).

Therefore, studying the JEP's legitimacy is important for transitional justice studies, as it contributes to verify whether "balanced justice" approaches designs are enough to improve democracy and reduce human rights violations. This study goes beyond the discussion of the best type of transitional justice mechanism to analyse the impact that its operation, its decisions, and its daily symbols have in the fulfilment of society's expectations.

Furthermore, it tries to adopt the suggestion Olsen et al. made in their book about having justice, fairness and rule of law as a measure of success, proposing some ways to measure them (2010, 161). This book suggests also adopting legitimacy as one important indicator of success for a transitional justice mechanism and proposes ways of measuring it, as will be explained in Chapter 4.

1.4.2 Studying a Mixed Approach for Conflict-Related Crimes

The JEP's case is also relevant for transitional justice studies because it applies a mixed approach to conflict-related crimes—combining the use of restorative and retributive justice. The States have not usually used this approach, and it might be an option to better help societies to heal trauma while effectively punishing the key perpetrators.

Historically, the States began using retribute justice to adjudicate grave human rights violations. The most iconic case is the International Military Tribunal in Nuremberg, commonly known as the "Nuremberg trials", where several former Nazi leaders were held accountable for their actions in World War II (Anna Myriam Roccatello and Gabriel Rojas 2020). Despite this landmark precedent, in general, countries have avoided the use of trials, with the rare exception of Argentina, which on 1985 famously had the "trial of the generals" of the dictatorship (1976–1983). When State held trials to sanction grave human rights violations, they often involved the participation of international courts. One example is that of the former Yugoslavia.

By 1994, the wars in former Yugoslavia had caused around 200,000–250,000 dead, 50,000 tortured and 20,000 raped, along with more than 3 million refugees. Considering that the local courts either were not effectively adjudicating these crimes or were supposedly holding biased trials, in 1993, the United Nations Security Council approved the creation of the International Criminal Tribunal for the Former Yugoslavia (ICTY) "with the purposes of contributing to the restoration of peace, punishing the offenders, and delivering justice to the victims" (Kutnjak Ivković and Hagan 2017, 200). Overall, the ICTY prosecuted and sentenced 79 individuals.

Progressively, societies have moved to more restorative approaches (Anna Myriam Roccatello and Gabriel Rojas 2020). The paradigmatic example is the South Africa's Truth and Reconciliation Commission, where amnesties were granted on the condition of contributing to provide truth. Others have used a mix of measures. For example, between 2001 and 2003, Peru's Commission for Truth and Reconciliation focused on highlighting the dignity of marginalised communities and the victims, while efforts to prosecute former dictator Alberto Fujimori (1990–2000) produced slower results.

The JEP's design combines both elements in a judicial system: a restorative approach for those who contribute to the victims' rights and a retributive response to those who do not. The ICTJ has considered that this approach "offers great promise in transitional justice contexts" (Anna Myriam Roccatello and Gabriel Rojas 2020). Unlike the retributive model, restorative processes can foster more participation from victims and perpetrators. By retaining some retributive elements, the JEP may offer more incentives to cooperate, satisfy international human rights standards, deter perpetrators who still are in positions of power from reoffending and demonstrate to a larger public that a transitional justice process does not equate to impunity, as it is typically perceived. Thus, studying the JEP's legitimacy is important to assess the society's acceptance of a promising mixed-approach system.

1.5 Importance of Studying the JEP's Legitimacy to Fulfil Its Objectives

Furthermore, legitimacy is essential to the fulfilment of the JEP's goals. The academic literature has consistently shown that trust in courts and support for them ensure their independence and is also related to the citizens' acceptance of the rulings (Botero 2020; Gibson and Caldeira 2003; Easton 1975). Legitimacy is also necessary to protect the rights of minorities or marginalised communities and hand down rulings that may be unpopular. Thus, if courts do not have a reservoir of trust and support, they may not have incentives to make contentious decisions (Forero-Alba and Rodríguez-Raga 2022, 191).

As Botero points out, legitimacy, or in her words, trust, may be even more important for transitional courts and recently created courts (2020, 302). Transitional courts usually operate in a polarised context, under the pressure of victims, political actors and social organisations, among other actors. Besides that, they have ambitious objectives that usually involve the reconciliation of a society, providing truth of events that happened decades before their operation, and fostering the transition to a peace context. Due to all these reasons, usually transitional justice Courts must rule on controversial and unpopular issues.

Specifically, in the JEP's case, legitimacy is very important to achieve its objectives. As was described above, the JEP's main purposes are to: "satisfy the victims' right to justice, providing truth to the Colombian society, protecting the victims' rights, contributing to achieving a stable and lasting peace, and taking decisions that ensure judicial certainty to those who participated in grave human rights violations" (Congress of the Republic of Colombia 2017). If the JEP lacks legitimacy, its decisions might be disobeyed by the authorities, the victims or those sentenced. What is more, the JEP rulings could foster polarisation instead of enhancing "a stable and lasting peace". Unsatisfied groups might suggest that decisions should be overruled and that cases should be adjudicated again by a different tribunal. For instance, in February 2024, as a result of an increased dissatisfaction with the JEP's operation that will be explained in Sect. 5.2.7, some notorious members of the FARC-EP proposed in a public letter the creation of a new Tribunal. Unlike the JEP, this judicial system would adjudicate the crimes committed by all the actors, even those perpetrated by armed groups that have ongoing peace conversations with the Petro Administration (Cindy A. Morales Castillo 2024). An illegitimate JEP could not provide legal certainty to those involved in grave human rights violations, and the victims' rights could be violated: suspected perpetrators would not cooperate with the JEP and much of the truth and reparations victims need could not be obtained, let alone the guarantees of non-recurrence in case the *comparecientes*[6] commit crimes again.

These scenarios are partially hypothetical because they have not completely occurred yet, but, as I have pointed out, some main actors like the former FARC-EP have started to express that the JEP has gone astray from what they signed and that they may disobey its rulings. This reinforces the importance of studying the JEP's legitimacy now. Highlighting the legitimacy's trade-offs and identifying the factors that affect it might be of use to JEP's judicial operators and policymakers to adopt changes to improve legitimacy. Given its independence and autonomy,

[6] There is not a suitable concept in English for the term "compareciente", which literally could mean "that who appears before the Court". Throughout this book "compareciente" would refer to any defendant whose case is adjudicated by the JEP due to mandatory jurisdiction (members of the FARC-EP and Armed Forces) or because they filed the case voluntarily (a civilian or a non-armed State agent).

the JEP can organise its operation within the legal framework to adopt relevant measures.

1.6 Academic Importance of Studying the JEP's Legitimacy

Probing the JEP's legitimacy is important for academia because studying the mass public attitudes regarding transitional justice judicial systems is an understudied area (Botero 2020, 302). Moreover, the creation of a new judicial system is a rare event, and there are few studies covering those initial years. This book endeavours to contribute to improve the understanding of these areas. To do so, I will draw on previous literature about the legitimacy of: (1) national courts (Gibson et al. 1998; Gibson and Caldeira 2003; Forero-Alba and Rodríguez-Raga 2022); (2) international courts (Allioui 2020; Voeten 2013; Shany 2014); (3) international transitional justice institutions (Kutnjak Ivković and Hagan 2017); and (4) the State in general (Beetham 2013; Coicaud 2002; Weber 2019), including the Latin American States.

Furthermore, the legitimacy of the JEP has been previously studied, especially in the first years of the JEP and usually addressing both the legal and sociological perspective (Maria del Pilar Bahamón and Harvey Danilo Suárez 2020; Gómez 2022; Iván Orozco Abad 2020; Valencia Valencia and Francés-Gómez 2018; Botero 2020; Mayans-Hermida et al. 2023). However, these papers and book sections are siloed. They do not reference each other. The discussions are varied, not integrated around a clear concept of legitimacy, and inconclusive in terms of assessing the JEP's legitimacy in general. This book is an attempt to connect the dots.

Drawing on Rawls and Habermas theories, Valencia Valencia and Francés-Gómez (2018) argued that the JEP was politically legitimate in its origin because: (a) it was created through deliberative processes; (b) it was the result of a reasonable pact for building a stable and lasting peace, instead of continuing a war that would kill thousands, while not having a clear winner; (c) it was supported by Colombia's most affected areas; and (d) it was endorsed by Congress. Furthermore, the fact that there was no alternative to reach the desirable outcomes in terms of adjudicating conflict-related crimes would also legitimate the JEP. Unlike this book, the authors did not analyse the JEP's operation, societal perceptions, and relied their findings solely on academic literature.

On the contrary, Botero (2020) examines public opinion regarding the JEP through an experimental study, putting a vast academic literature on the legitimacy of high courts and transitional justice mechanisms in dialogue with the JEP's case. Drawing on experimental evidence, she concludes that, in a hypothetical case where the JEP handed down a restorative sentence, respondents were less likely to support the decision and expressed lower levels of trust in the institution. Conversely, trust in the JEP and support for its rulings increased when the sanction involved imprisonment. Whether the accused was member of the FARC-EP or the Armed Forces did not have a significant effect on the citizens' perception of the JEP.

Given that the JEP will potentially sanction perpetrators with more restorative sanctions than retributive, Botero expected that, in the medium term, consistent low support for such decisions would impact general trust in this relatively young judicial institution.

Moreover, Mayans-Hermida et al. (2023) conducted 44 interviews to key stakeholders—victims, victims' attorneys, international actors, JEP clerks, among others—to understand their perceptions on the special sanctions, which potentially impacts their support for the JEP. The authors confirmed the assumptions of some of the Peace negotiators and JEP designers: most participants perceived restorative sanctions as a way to repair the inflicted damage in some way, reintegrate offenders into society, restoring coexistence. Yet, only few thought that these measures were a punishment, but rather an alternative measure to jail.

Bahamón and Suárez (2020), Orozco (2020), and Gómez (2022) highlighted how several sectors do not accept the JEP as a legitimate institution and suggested some ways of achieving legitimacy. The first claimed that the JEP's legitimacy depends on the correspondence between the JEP's principles, proceedings and results, and the constitutional values, ends and principles underpinned in the Colombian rule of law.

The second stressed the coordination and administrative challenges the JEP might face in its operation. Orozco recalled the political struggle around the JEP's design and implementation, as he pointed out some favourable elements for the JEP—the international community strongly supported its operation, several Colombian institutions approved its creation, and the diverse origin of the JEP's justices could turn into an advantage. He also argued that, to improve its legitimacy, the JEP should produce early results, implement a strong communication strategy, position the JEP's judicial truth and importance, and encourage the victims' participation in the proceedings, ensuring equal participation among the different sectors.

Gómez, in turn, proposed a theoretical framework to explain the political disputes around the JEP, drawing on Bourdieu's sociological theory. He argued that transitional justice is a "field in which diverse political, institutional and social actors with different levels of power and experiences struggle to defend their approaches to understanding the political conflict, how to reach justice, and how to protect the victims' rights" (2022, 15). In his opinion, transitional justice mechanisms and practices do not constitute a consensus, but a "space of social conflict". Gómez embraces a constructivist approach, viewing transitional justice as an expression of societal dynamics that could also potentially create social realities and prompt social transformations.

As said above, this book is an attempt to connect the dots. As most of the existing literature, it describes the political disputes around the JEP's legitimacy. However, it does suggests a clear definition of legitimacy, focusing on sociological legitimacy—"the right a judicial institution has to make judicial decisions, according to social perceptions and beliefs". Given that the JEP is an already established institution, sociological legitimacy is the most suitable for this case. It goes beyond political and legal disputes, focusing on the correspondence between the JEP's operations and the societal expectations and values. Following Gómez's constructivist approach, the JEP's practices might align or misalign with these expectations, impacting success and acceptance among society. In a few words, the JEP's operation has a direct impact in its own legitimacy.

Furthermore, this study is the first piece of literature to rely on existing surveys and fieldwork data, especially on a large number of interviews, to study the JEP's legitimacy. Apart from the seminal work by Botero (2020), no other piece of literature has drawn on the literature on the legitimacy of high courts and transitional justice mechanisms to study the JEP's case.

Lastly, this book develops a method to assess the legitimacy of judicial transitional justice mechanisms, taking into account the factors explained by Orozco and Botero's and Mayans-Hermida's findings. Explaining this process can tell that a holistic design is not enough to ensure the success of a transitional justice mechanism. Operation is equally important and sometimes even more so.

1.7 Book Overview

To study the JEP's sociological legitimacy, Chapter 2 explains the methods I use in this book. In Chapter 3, I present a relevant historical background to the JEP in order to better understand the development of such an institution.

Chapter 4 lays the conceptual framework. It establishes: (1) the concepts I use to explain and gauge the JEP's sociological legitimacy; (2) the factors that the literature has identified that erode or strengthen the legitimacy of a judicial institution, and (3) the signs that may alert the presence or absence of such factors. The last part of this chapter explains how to measure the JEP's sociological legitimacy by assessing the signs of the factors on a scale. Chapter 5 carries out the analysis. It adapts the conceptual framework to the case of the JEP, thereby assessing its legitimacy.

Finally, Chapter 6 provides some reflections on the findings and their implications for the future of the JEP and similar mechanisms in other contexts of massive human rights violations.

References

Allioui, Samira. 2020. "Legitimacy and International Courts." *International Journal for Court Administration* 11 (1). https://doi.org/10.36745/ijca.288.

Anna Myriam Roccatello and Gabriel Rojas. 2020. *A Mixed Approach to International Crimes: The Retributive and Restorative Justice Procedures of Colombia's Special Jurisdiction for Peace*. International Center for Transitional Justice. https://www.ictj.org/sites/default/files/ICTJ_Report_Colombia_MixedProcedures.pdf.

Auto 019 de 2021 (Special Jurisdiction for Peace January 26, 2021). https://www.jep.gov.co/Sala-de-Prensa/Documents/CASO%2001%20TOMA%20DE%20REHENES/Auto%20No.%2019%20de%202021.pdf?csf=1&e=16bYs0.

BBC News Mundo. 2010. "BBC Mundo - América Latina - Corte Constitucional de Colombia dice 'no' a la reelección de Álvaro Uribe." British Broadcasting Corporation, February 27. 10/02/100226_2238_uribe_reeleccion_colombia_constitucional_irm.shtml.

BBC News Mundo. 2016a. "Colombia: el Congreso aprueba el nuevo acuerdo de paz con las FARC y las divisiones se trasladan a las presidenciales de 2018." *BBC News Mundo*, December 1. https://www.bbc.com/mundo/noticias-america-latina-38165978.

BBC News Mundo. 2016b. "Colombia: ganó el 'No' en el plebiscito por los acuerdos de paz con las FARC." *BBC News Mundo*, October 2. https://www.bbc.com/mundo/noticias-america-latina-37537187.

Beetham, David. 2013. *The Legitimation of Power*, 2nd ed. Political Analysis (Palgrave Macmillan (Firm)): Palgrave Macmillan.

Bermúdez Liévano, Andrés, ed. 2018. *Los debates de La Habana: una mirada desde adentro*. Fondo de Capital Humano para la Transición Colombiana, Instituto para las Transiciones Integrales (IFIT).

Biblioteca Abierta del Proceso de Paz colombiano. 2021. "BAPP - Biblioteca Abierta del Proceso de Paz colombiano." *¿Cuándo? El proceso de paz en el tiempo*, March 29. https://bapp.com.co/cuando/.

Borda, Fals, Germán Guzmán. Orlando, and Eduardo Umaña. 1962. *La Violencia En Colombia*. Bogotá: Tercer Mundo.

Botero, Sandra. 2020. Trust in Colombia's Justicia Especial Para La Paz: Experimental Evidence. *Journal of Politics in Latin America* 12 (3): 300–322. https://doi.org/10.1177/1866802X20959509.

Canal Institucional de Colombia. 2020. "Las razones de la CPI para decir que JEP es referente mundial." Canal Institucional TV, November 3. https://www.canalinstitucional.tv/noticias/jep-es-ejemplo-internacional-segun-corte-penal-internacional.

Cindy A. Morales Castillo. 2024. "Exsecretariado de FARC propone 'tribunal de cierre' por presuntos incumplimientos de JEP." Paz y Memoria. *El Espectador*, February 24. https://www.elespectador.com/colombia-20/paz-y-memoria/exsecretariado-de-farc-propondra-a-petro-un-tribunal-de-cierre-que-podria-eliminar-a-la-jep/.

Coicaud, Jean-Marc. 2002. *Legitimacy and Politics: A Contribution to the Study of Political Right and Political Responsibility*. With David Ames Curtis and Cambridge University Press. Cambridge Core. University Press. https://ezproxy-prd.bodleian.ox.ac.uk/login?url=10.1017/CBO9780511490200.

Congress of the Republic of Colombia. 2017. "Constitutional Reform 1 of 2017." April 4. http://www.secretariasenado.gov.co/senado/basedoc/acto_legislativo_01_2017.html.

De la Calle Lombana, Humberto. 2019. *Revelaciones al Final de Una Guerra: Testimonio Del Jefe Negociador Del Gobierno Colombiano En La Habana*. DEBATE.

Desjardins, Jeff. 2019. "Mapped: The World's Oldest Democracies." World Economic Forum, August 8. https://www.weforum.org/stories/2019/08/countries-are-the-worlds-oldest-democracies/.

Easton, David. 1975. A Re-Assessment of the Concept of Political Support. *British Journal of Political Science* 5 (4): 435–457. https://doi.org/10.1017/S0007123400008309.

El Colombiano. 2010. "La de Uribe, una histórica popularidad." El Colombiano, August 5. https://www.elcolombiano.com/historico/la_de_uribe_una_historica_popularidad-HVEC_99428.

El Espectador. 2020. "La cuestionable estrategia de campaña del No." Text. ELESPECTADOR.COM, March 24. https://www.elespectador.com/politica/la-cuestionable-estrategia-de-campana-del-no-article-658862/.

El Espectador. 2024. "Corte Constitucional rechaza por segunda vez demanda del exministro Yesid Reyes." Judicial. *El Espectador* (Bogotá), November 1. https://www.elespectador.com/judicial/por-segunda-vez-corte-constitucional-rechazo-demanda-del-exministro-yesid-reyes-noticias-de-hoy/.

El País. 2016. "Uribe rechaza el nuevo acuerdo de paz entre el Gobierno y las FARC y pide un nuevo plebiscito." América Colombia. *El País* (Madrid), November 22. https://elpais.com/internacional/2016/11/22/colombia/1479819217_374727.html.

Ferry, Stephen. 2012. *Violentology: A Manual of the Colombian Conflict*. 1st ed. Umbrage.

Figueroa Cordero, Ronald Javier. 2022. "Relatos de 'Todo Lo Malo': El Caso de Chulavita, Memoria Sobre La Violencia." Universidad de los Andes. http://hdl.handle.net/1992/60723.

Forero-Alba, Sofía, and Juan Carlos Rodríguez-Raga. 2022. "Courting Judicial Legitimacy: An Experimental Study of the Colombian Constitutional Court." In *The Limits of Judicialization*, 1st ed., edited by Sandra Botero, Daniel M. Brinks, and Ezequiel A. Gonzalez-Ocantos. Cambridge University Press. https://doi.org/10.1017/9781009093859.007.

Gibson, James L., and Gregory A. Caldeira. 2003. Defenders of Democracy? Legitimacy, Popular Acceptance, and the South African Constitutional Court. *The Journal of Politics* 65 (1): 1–30. https://doi.org/10.1111/1468-2508.t01-1-00001.

Gibson, James, Gregory Caldeira, and Vanessa Baird. 1998. On the Legitimacy of National High Courts. *The American Political Science Review* 92 (June): 343. https://doi.org/10.2307/2585668.

Gómez, Gabriel Ignacio. 2022. "Political Conflicts over the JEP: A Sociolegal Perspective." In *Transitional Justice in Colombia: The Special Jurisdiction for Peace [Electronic Resource]*, edited by Kai Ambos and Stefan Peters, with Susann Aboueldahab. Studien Zu Lateinamerika; Volume 44. Nomos. https://directory.doabooks.org/handle/20.500.12854/81931.

Grupo de Memoria Histórica. 2013. *¡Basta ya! Colombia, memorias de guerra y dignidad: informe general*. Segunda edición corregida. Centro Nacional de Memoria Histórica.

Guevara, Carolina. 2011. Independencia Judicial: El Caso de La Corte Suprema de Justicia Colombiana. *Revista De Derecho*, 35: 145–179.

Gutiérrez Sanín, Francisco. 2020. *¿Un nuevo ciclo de la guerra en Colombia?* DEBATE.

Infobae. 2021. "'Perdió el plebiscito, es impuesta por las Farc y sesgada': nueva arremetida de Uribe contra la JEP." infobae, March 31. https://www.infobae.com/america/colombia/2021/03/31/perdio-el-plebiscito-es-impuesta-por-las-farc-y-sesgada-nueva-arremetida-de-uribe-contra-la-jep/.

Infobae. 2024. "Álvaro Uribe aseguró que la JEP está en deuda con los soldados: 'Recibieron el trato de ejército de matones.'" infobae, March 5. https://www.infobae.com/colombia/2024/03/05/alvaro-uribe-aseguro-que-la-jep-esta-en-deuda-con-los-soldados-colombianos-recibieron-el-trato-de-ejercito-de-matones/.

Interamerican Court of Human Rights. 2012. *Sentencia Corte IDH Masacre el Mozote Vs El Salvador 2012.* https://corteidh.or.cr/docs/casos/articulos/seriec_252_esp.pdf.

International Criminal Court. 2021. "ICC Prosecutor, Mr Karim A. A. Khan QC, Concludes the Preliminary Examination of the Situation in Colombia with a Cooperation Agreement with the Government Charting the next Stage in Support of Domestic Efforts to Advance Transitional Justice." October 28. https://www.icc-cpi.int/news/icc-prosecutor-mr-karim-khan-qc-concludes-preliminary-examination-situation-colombia.

Iván Orozco Abad. 2020. "Sobre Algunos Desafíos Conceptuales y de Legitimidad de La JEP." In *La JEP Vista Por Sus Jueces (2018–2019)*, edited by Jurisdicción Especial para la Paz. Jurisdicción Especial para la Paz. https://www.jep.gov.co/Documents/LA%20JEP%20VISTA%20POR%20SUS%20JUEVES.pdf.

JEP Government Board. 2024. "Acuerdo 7 de 2024." February 16. https://www.jep.gov.co/organosgobierno/Acuerdo%20AOG%20007%20de%202024.pdf.

Justice Subcommission of the 2016 Colombian Peace Agreement. 2015. "Subcomisión de Justicia. Bases Compartidas." Biblioteca Abierta del Proceso de Paz colombiano, July 27. https://bapp.com.co/archivos/1.01.0917.pdf.

Kutnjak Ivković, Sanja, and John Hagan. 2017. "The Legitimacy of International Courts: Victims' Evaluations of the ICTY and Local Courts in Bosnia and Herzegovina." *European Journal of Criminology* (London, England) 14 (2): 200–220. https://doi.org/10.1177/1477370816649625.

Leongómez, Eduardo Pizarro. 2015. "Una Lectura Múltiple y Pluralista de La Historia." *Contribución al Entendimiento Del Conflicto Armado En Colombia*, 3–94.

Maria del Pilar Bahamón and Harvey Danilo Suárez. 2020. "Legitimidad Por Vía de Juridicidad: Narrativas En Disputa Sobre La Jurisdicción Especial Para La Paz Como Mecanismo de Justicia Restaurativa En Entornos de Impunidad y Polarización." In *La JEP Vista Por Sus Jueces (2018–2019).*

Mauricio Villamil. 2025. "Corte Constitucional analiza demanda que cuestiona ampliación de investigados por parte de la JEP con la 'Senit 5.'" Colombia. *Infobae*, May 6. https://www.infobae.com/colombia/2025/05/06/corte-constitucional-analiza-demanda-que-cuestiona-ampliacion-de-investigados-por-parte-de-la-jep-con-la-senit-5/.

Mayans-Hermida, Beatriz E. Barbora Holá, and Catrien Bijleveld. 2023. "Between Impunity and Justice? Exploring Stakeholders' Perceptions of Colombia's Special Sanctions (Sanciones Propias) for International Crimes." *International Journal of Transitional Justice*, May 19, ijad009. https://doi.org/10.1093/ijtj/ijad009.

Melo, Jorge Orlando. 2021. *Colombia: una historia mínima: una mirada integral al país*. Crítica.

National Government of Colombia and FARC-EP. 2012. "Acuerdo General Para La Terminación Del Conflicto y La Construcción de Una Paz Estable y Duradera." Biblioteca Abierta del Proceso de Paz colombiano, August 26. https://bapp.com.co/archivos/1.03.0058.pdf.

Olsen, Tricia D., Leigh A. Payne, and Andrew G. Reiter. 2010. *Transitional Justice in Balance: Comparing Processes, Weighing Efficacy*. U.S. Institute of Peace.

Red+ Noticias. 2023. "Los tradicionales jefes guerrilleros de las Farc que han muerto." Red+ Noticias, July 6. https://redmas.com.co/Los-tradicionales-jefes-guerrilleros-de-las-Farc-que-han-muerto-t202307060001.html.

Romero-Prieto, Julio Enrique, and Adolfo Meisel-Roca. 2019. "Análisis Demográfico de La Violencia En Colombia." *Cuadernos de Historia Económica; No. 50*.

Sánchez, Nelson Camilo, Leigh A. Payne, Gabriel Pereira, Laura Bernal, Daniel Marín, and Miguel Barboza. 2018. *Cuentas Claras: El Papel de la Comisión de la Verdad en la Develación de la Responsabilidad de Empresas en el Conflicto Armado Colombiano*. 1st ed. Dejusticia Series. Centro de Estudios de Derecho, Justicia y Sociedad.

Santos, Juan Manuel. 2019. *La Batalla Por La Paz*. Grupo Planeta - Colombia.

Shany, Yuval. 2014. *Assessing the Effectiveness of International Courts*. Oxford University Press. https://doi.org/10.1093/acprof:oso/9780199643295.001.0001.

Truth Commission of Colombia. 2022a. "Cifras de la Comisión de la Verdad presentadas junto con el Informe Final." June 11. https://web.comisiondelaverdad.co/actualidad/noticias/principales-cifras-comision-de-la-verdad-informe-final.

Truth Commission of Colombia. 2022b. *No matarás: relato histórico del conflicto armado interno en Colombia*. Primera edición. Hay futuro si hay verdad, Tomo 3,3. Comisión de la Verdad.

Valencia Valencia, Paula Andrea, and Pedro Francés-Gómez. 2018. "Legitimidad de la Jurisdicción Especial para la Paz." *Revista de Paz y Conflictos* 11 (1): 105–33. https://doi.org/10.30827/revpaz.v11i1.6027.

Villar Borda, Leopoldo. 2020. "El 'golpe de opinión' que decepcionó a Colombia." El Tiempo, June 12. https://www.eltiempo.com/colombia/otras-ciudades/dictadura-de-rojas-pinilla-golpe-de-opinion-que-decepciono-a-colombia-506522.

Voeten, Erik. 2013. Public Opinion and the Legitimacy of International Courts. *Theoretical Inquiries in Law (Tel Aviv)* 14 (2): 411–436. https://doi.org/10.1515/til-2013-021.

Weber, Max. 2019. *Economy and Society: A New Translation*. With Keith Tribe. Ebook Central. Harvard University Press. https://ezproxy-prd.bodleian.ox.ac.uk/login?url=https://ebookcentral.proquest.com/lib/oxford/detail.action?docID=5715885.

CHAPTER 2

Data and Methods

Abstract This section describes the data and the methodology used. The book is a case study: it explores to what extent existing theories are useful to explain the JEP's sociological legitimacy. When theories fail to do so, I propose alternative explanations. The method of analysis is process tracing, following Bennett and Checkel's definition as "the analysis of evidence on processes, sequences, and conjunctures of events within a case for the purposes of either developing or testing hypotheses about causal mechanisms that might causally explain the case" (2014, 7). In other words, this book will analyse interviews, polls, news and hearings, among other data, with the aim of testing the hypothesis about the causal mechanisms that explain the legitimacy of the JEP. The hypothesis is that the JEP responds to the same processes of construction of legitimacy of any judicial institution. The chapter also explores potential ethics and ethical dilemmas and data limitations.

Keywords Process tracing · Research methods · Interviews · Ethical dilemmas · Mixed methods · Research on Courts

N. Zuluaga Afanador, *The Sociological Legitimacy of the Special Jurisdiction for Peace of Colombia*, St Antony's Series,
https://doi.org/10.1007/978-3-032-21912-1_2

In essence, this book is a case study. It uses the JEP's case to test what the literature has said about the construction of legitimacy in judicial institutions. As described above, legal regulations and practices can transform the social perception of an institution (Gómez 2022). Similarly, factors like the loyalty for a Court, the acceptance of some of its decisions or the salience of the Court's practices and jurisdiction may impact its legitimacy capital (Gibson et al. 1998). Over time, this can change. I want to probe to what extent existing legitimacy theories are useful to explain the JEP's sociological legitimacy. When they fail to explain a particular aspect, I will posit alternative explanations. By delving into how much the theory is applicable to the JEP, I endeavour to provide ideas of an unstudied case: the construction of sociological legitimacy in transitional justice judicial systems.

2.1 Method: Process Tracing

The method I will use to verify the legitimacy theories suitability for the JEP's case is process tracing. It is the most suitable for the available data and the case. It allows for understanding the middle steps in the construction of the outcome (sociological legitimacy), using a wide variety of qualitative methods, such as interviews, social media analysis and participant observation and testing the legitimacy theories.

I adopt Bennett and Checkel's definition of process tracing as "the analysis of evidence on processes, sequences, and conjunctures of events within a case for the purposes of either developing or testing hypotheses about causal mechanisms that might causally explain the case" (2014, 7). This book will analyse interviews, polls, news and hearings, among other data, with the aim of testing the hypothesis about the causal mechanisms that explain the legitimacy of the JEP. The hypothesis is that the JEP responds to the same processes of construction of legitimacy of any judicial institution.

The spatial and topical domain are clear: the case involves the sociological legitimacy of the Special Jurisdiction for Peace of Colombia, yet the temporal sphere must be clarified. I researched the subject between 2016—when the Peace Agreement with the FARC began to be discussed on the eve of the referendum—and May 2024, when many of the former JEP supporters, among them the ex-top FARC commanders and several National Government peace negotiators presented substantial critiques to the JEP.

However, as an operating institution, the JEP's legitimacy can be assessed at any moment and is expected to change. That is why I assess a period of time and propose a method anyone could use in future.

In this analysis, the dependent variable is the JEP's legitimacy, while the independent variables are the factors identified by the academic literature as impacting judicial legitimacy: (1) diffuse and specific support; (2) the Court's salience; (3) its age; and (4) the obedience to its rulings.

The proposal causal chain suggests that the JEP's legitimacy responds to changes in public attitudes and institutional performance. Specifically, legitimacy increases or declines as (1) citizens demonstrate loyalty to the JEP—or withdrawn their support from it—; (2) as they endorse or reject its decisions; and (3) as they understand or remain unaware of its structure, objective and practices. Additionally, legitimacy is shaped over time (4), as the JEP hands down more decisions and exposes the society to its symbols. The degree to which state authorities and individuals obey or disobey the JEP's rulings also plays a crucial role (5).

In sum, the JEP's legitimacy is determined by the citizen's loyalty to the JEP, their support for its rulings, the extent to which individuals understand its structure and mixed approach, the passing of time and the obedience of its rulings.

2.2 Data

I employ triangulation of sources to generate the data necessary to understand the JEP's sociological legitimacy. Specifically, I will use: (1) the 43 interviews I conducted during fieldwork; (2) the participant observation of a hearing of acknowledgement of responsibility at Yopal between September 18 and 20, 2023; (3) relevant academic literature on the JEP; (4) social media; and (5) news and several opinion pieces.

Regarding the fieldwork I conducted, interviews are important for tracing the process of interest because they provide data that is very difficult to obtain otherwise—changes in the perception of the JEP, believes about restorative justice, information about people who might influence their support for the JEP, internal practices or specific proceedings. Through an interview, a participant can better explain the nuances of their relations with the JEP, unlike in a survey.

Furthermore, interviews are an opportunity to create a trustworthy space, where people could freely express their thoughts and emotions, providing more reliable data. I decided then to prioritise in-person meetings. This is particularly important in Colombia, a country where people might refrain from talking about issues that might be controversial, even if it is for educational purposes. Being vocal might entail some risks. Another reason I had to encourage in-person meetings is that they provide more opportunities to observe non-verbal language and, thus, have more data.

The period of fieldwork was between June and September 2023, when I conducted 43 semi-structured interviews in total. Interviews are important for tracing the process of interest because they account for legitimacy changes over time, unveil perceptions on the JEP, and convey citizens' expectations over the JEP and the values at stake.

When I talked with participants, I started asking them general open questions about the past, present, and future of the JEP's legitimacy. To begin with, I talked them through my definition of legitimacy and inquired about their notion of this concept.

To that point, they had to assess the JEP's legitimacy in the present, past and future and identify the factors that could strengthen or erode that legitimacy. In that process, I asked them about the influence of the legitimacy factors identified by the literature: (1) the JEP's salience; (2) the extent to which people understand the JEP's structure and operation; (3) the support for several JEP rulings, some of them controversial, like the Santrich decision, which will be explained in Sect. 5.1.3.1; and (4) their perceptions about the JEP's hearings, which are useful to expose citizens to symbols and restorative justice. I also inquired to what extent the passage of time impacts the JEP's legitimacy.

All these questions helped me to understand to what extent the theories I was verifying were applicable to the case in interest. Many of them made sense in the JEP's context, but, as I was conducting more interviews, I realised that participants consistently pointed out new relevant factors. For example, I acknowledged that the extent to which the JEP offers equal treatment to FARC-EP and Armed Forces Members, and the fact that the JEP practices could offer new information to the victims were factors that impacted people's support to the JEP's decisions.

As far as the interviewees are concerned, I sought to do elite interviews, namely accessing individuals who might influence the JEP's operation or its perception by public opinion. In this point I followed Harvey's definition, according to which individuals belonging to an elite are "those who hold important social networks, social capital and strategic positions within social structures because they are better able to exert influence" (2011, 433).

I opted for selecting those who represented different key sectors of society and diverse ideologies, seeking a comprehensive understanding of the JEP's sociological legitimacy. Thus, out of the 43 interviewees: (a) 12 individuals worked in the JEP either as directors of administrative offices or justices, and some had been Presidents of the JEP; (b) 9 had actively participated in the JEP's proceedings either as victims or victims' attorneys; (c) 7 were intellectuals that had studied and written extensively about the JEP, transitional justice or the legitimacy of institutions in Colombia; (d) 6 had openly criticised, defended or supported the JEP, including the former President Iván Duque and the former top commander of the FARC-EP, Rodrigo Londoño Echeverri; (e) 6 had followed the JEP as news journalists or cartoonists; (f) 2 worked as key officers for the government; and (g) one was an important international figure involved in supporting the peace process.

In other words, I covered different sectors of society related to the JEP: victims, intellectuals, politicians, JEP officials, international actors and workers of the media industry. I also considered a gender perspective. Although less represented, 15 interviewees were women, whereas 28 were male.

Most of the interviewees were in Bogotá (32), although 4 were in Medellín, 2 were in Oxford, one was in Pereira (Colombia), one was in Switzerland and one was in Virginia (United States). At the same time, I sought to maintain a territorial perspective because Colombia is a very diverse country in terms of territory, culture and the armed conflict took place mostly in rural areas. Consequently, within the limits of funding and time, I attempted to include regional perspectives.

I observed a hearing in Yopal, a city with more than 168,000 inhabitants in the northeastern area of Colombia, close to the border with Venezuela, and I contacted victims and attorneys in Medellín and Putumayo. I also attempted to arrange the participation of a group of victims of sexual violence who live in Putumayo, an area in the Southwestern part of Colombia that is deeply affected by drug trafficking, paramilitaries and lack of State presence. Despite having the option of participating anonymously and virtually, they refused to do so, due to the associated risks. This situation shows that insecurity is still a large concern in some areas of the country, as Julia Zulver has described for women mobilising for gender justice in Putumayo (Zulver 2022).

Following a discussion with my supervisor about the fact that I had previously worked at the JEP and acknowledging potential biases I will explain in the following section, I selected some of the candidates using previous social networking I had built personally, either working at the JEP (2018–2020, 2021–2022) or as a Research Officer at the University of Essex (2020–2021). After interviewing an individual, I always asked whether they thought I could interview somebody else, and thus I recruited more participants through snowball sampling.

As I was conducting fieldwork, the question of when to stop began to rise, similarly to what Bennett and Checkel have posited. According to them, a researcher should stop "when repetition occurs" (Bennett and Checkel 2014, 28); this means, when following one stream of evidence "becomes so repetitive that gathering more of that same kind of evidence has a low probability of revising their estimate of the likely accuracy of alternative explanations" (Bennett and Checkel 2014, 28). This occurred after I interviewed all the abovementioned individuals.

Apart from conducting interviews, I included a participant observation of a hearing that was held in Yopal from September 18 to 20, 2023, after being authorised by the Department of Restorative of the JEP. In this event, 21 members of the Armed Forces (among them one general), 1 agent of the State and 2 civilians acknowledged their responsibility for the killing and disappearance of 303 individuals who were presented as FARC casualties.

I understood participant observation as "the process enabling researchers to learn about the activities of the people under study in the natural setting through observing and participating in those activities" (Kawulich 2005). Accordingly, I paid close attention to the interactions between victims, perpetrators, and judges during the hearings. I also registered the setting of the hearings, including the symbolic objects employed by participants—such as candles, banners, restored vases, among others—as well as the sequencing and timing of interventions.

One illustrative example is the use of restored vases, created by the victims through a process facilitated by the JEP. These vases were assembled by glueing together broken clay pieces, inspired by the Japanese art of Kintsugi, which emphasises the beauty of repair. This symbolic act entailed a collective effort to restore dignity fractured by past violence. The completed objects were displayed at the Yopal hearing's scenario, as shown in Image 2.1.

Image 2.1 Stage in Yopal hearing (*Source* Author's own photograph)

Overall, I was attentive to understanding how these symbolic elements and ritual practices contributed to wither building or eroding the JEP's perceived legitimacy.

I also conducted media studies. I followed news related to the JEP in El Espectador, La Silla Vacía and Semana. The first two are news outlets usually in favour of the Peace Agreement and the latter is arguably the most critical.

To delve into the JEP critiques and veto actors, I systematically analysed the content related to the JEP on Semana's website. I reviewed 5,720 results from March 2018 to April 2024, searching for "JEP" using the Semana website's search engine.

2.3 Ethics and Ethical Dilemmas

As I was preparing and conducting fieldwork, I asked myself to what extent I should disclose my previous working relationship with the JEP. I worked at the JEP between November 2018 and November 2020 and between August 2021 and August 2022. In a political context as sensitive as Colombia's, I wondered whether opponents to the JEP might mistrust me, preventing them from replying honestly, openly and directly. After discussing that issue with my supervisor, I decided to disclose my previous affiliation to the JEP to enhance trust and reaffirm that I understood the JEP's complexity. Being empathetic and having deep knowledge of the institution, I was more suited to understand their critiques. In general, I found that I could build trusting connections with the interviewees, regardless of my professional background.

Additionally, I discussed my potential biases and concluded that I could present a balanced analysis of the JEP. Having worked at the institution, I could have had a bias in favour of it. However, knowing also the internal dynamics and flaws, I could also develop an informed criticism against it. Moreover, I was no longer connected to the JEP and did not have significant communication with my former employers.

Another issue that I tried to mitigate was security risks for myself and the interviewees. I met with all the interviewees in public places—coffee shops and restaurants—and when they were in other cities or it was difficult to meet in person, we talked via a meeting on Microsoft Teams. I also stressed to the participants that they could talk anonymously, and 8 did so.

2.4 Limitations

The data has two relevant limitations: the sample of the interviews is limited and not representative, and most of the data are qualitative. The quantitative data are opinion polls that assess favourable opinions of the JEP and trust in the JEP, proxies of the JEP's legitimacy (Invamer 2024; Rodríguez-Raga 2023). Given the time and funding limitations, conducting surveys on the topic was impossible.

In terms of the interviews, perpetrators, Afro-Colombians, indigenous people, members of the LGBT+ community and inhabitants of regions outside of Bogotá are underrepresented. The main reason is the lack of time and economic resources. Further research should also explore the opinion of all these individuals.

As the Peace Agreement acknowledges, indigenous and afrodescendant communities were so deeply affected by the internal armed conflict that the Peace Agreement established that the JEP should have a gender and an ethnic approach (Colombian Government and FARC-EP 2016, 4, 124). Following that mandate, the JEP opened the macro-cases 2, 4, 5 and 9.[1] In particular, these macro-cases examine the crimes committed in areas where a large share of the population identifies as an ethnic minority, like Tumaco, Ricaurte and Barbacoas, in the Southwest of Colombia (case 2), Urabá, Northwestern area of Colombia, close to the border with Panama (case 4), North of Cauca and South of Valle del Cauca, Western area of Colombia (case 5), and the case 9 examines all crimes committed against ethnic peoples and their territories that are not studied in other cases. As I previously suggested, exploring the different perspectives across regions and between urban and rural contexts is also essential to understanding the JEP's legitimacy in such a diverse country as Colombia.

Although those communities might not be represented in the interviews, I was mindful of the importance of considering their visions and opinions: when possible, I questioned the interviewees about the different perspectives individuals from the underrepresented communities might have. I also sought to find narratives of the underrepresented groups in the media.

As I stated before, the other limitation of the data is that most of it is qualitative rather than quantitative. This poses a challenge when it comes to trying to make generalisable assertions out of the analysis. How can I ascertain that the perceptions of the sample of people I interviewed represent the perceptions of a country of more than 50 million people? Certainly, it is not possible to make that assumption.

However, the analysis of this book remains valid and valuable because the sources are substantial and conclusions may provide indications of the JEP's legitimacy and the relationship between Colombian society—or at least many of its sectors—and the JEP. Further research could probe those indications by conducting polls and quantitative analysis, as Gibson and Caldeira did for the case of the South African Constitutional Court (2003) or the US and European High Courts (1998).

To summarise, even though the sample of interviews is limited, I tried to offset such a limitation by asking interviewees about underrepresented groups and by looking for information on those constituencies' beliefs in the media. I did my best to use the available quantitative data. The most complete source was the Americas Barometer, a survey project by

[1] Macro-cases are the investigations the JEP has opened to examine thousands of facts in order to identify patterns of victimisation and those "most responsible" for executing them.

the Vanderbilt University's Latin America Public Opinion Project that has consulted people's opinions on democracy and governance across the Americas since 2004. In the case of Colombia, it asked the participants about their perceptions on the JEP in issues like restorative justice, trust and the accomplishment of the JEP's objectives in 2018 and 2023.

I complemented these data with surveys that were conducted regularly by the Colombian polling company Invamer on the favourable or unfavourable image of several public institutions (Invamer 2024). Further research might probe this book' conclusions by studying the perceptions of underrepresented communities and by analysing the available polls related to the JEP's legitimacy.

References

Bennett, Andrew, and Jeffrey T. Checkel. 2014. "Process Tracing: From Philosophical Roots to Best Practices." In *Process Tracing*, 1st ed., edited by Andrew Bennett and Jeffrey T. Checkel. Cambridge University Press. https://doi.org/10.1017/CBO9781139858472.003.

Colombian Government and FARC-EP. 2016. "Peace Agreement 2016." November 26. https://www.peaceagreements.org/wview/1845/Final%20Agreement%20to%20End%20the%20Armed%20Conflict%20and%20Build%20a%20Stable%20and%20Lasting%20Peace.

Gibson, James L., and Gregory A. Caldeira. 2003. Defenders of Democracy? Legitimacy, Popular Acceptance, and the South African Constitutional Court. *The Journal of Politics* 65 (1): 1–30. https://doi.org/10.1111/1468-2508.t01-1-00001.

Gibson, James, Gregory Caldeira, and Vanessa Baird. 1998. On the Legitimacy of National High Courts. *The American Political Science Review* 92 (June): 343. https://doi.org/10.2307/2585668.

Gómez, Gabriel Ignacio. 2022. "Political Conflicts over the JEP: A Sociolegal Perspective." In *Transitional Justice in Colombia: The Special Jurisdiction for Peace [Electronic Resource]*, edited by Kai Ambos and Stefan Peters, with Susann Aboueldahab. Studien Zu Lateinamerika; Volume 44. Nomos. https://directory.doabooks.org/handle/20.500.12854/81931.

Harvey, William S. 2011. Strategies for Conducting Elite Interviews. *Qualitative Research* 11 (4): 431–441. https://doi.org/10.1177/1468794111404329.

Invamer. 2024. "Encuesta Invamer Febrero 2024." February. https://caracoltv.brightspotcdn.com/2c/ae/5173738245abb2e043034a0c173a/encuesta-invamer-poll-febrero-2024.pdf.

Kawulich, Barbara B. 2005. "Participant Observation as a Data Collection Method." *Forum: Qualitative Social Research / Qualitative Sozialforschung* 6 (2): 1–22. Business Source Ultimate.

Rodríguez-Raga, Juan Carlos. 2023. "El Barómetro de Las Américas Toma El Pulso de La Democracia En Colombia." In *Pulso de La Democracia En Colombia: 2023*. Barómetro de Las Américas. https://www.vanderbilt.edu/lapop/colombia/ABCOL2023-Pulso-de-la-democracia-final-20240403.pdf.

Zulver, Julia. 2022. *High-Risk Feminism in Colombia: Women's Mobilization in Violent Contexts*. Rutgers University Press.

CHAPTER 3

Historical Background

Abstract This chapter elaborates on the historical background of the JEP. It briefly explains the JEP's origins, its design and the selection of the justice and their staff. The Section reports the extent of victimisation during the Colombian internal armed conflict, the difficulties of adjudicating these crimes through the ordinary justice system and the scope of the JEP's operation. Then, it describes the main elements of the JEP's operation: the macro-cases (cases to investigate and identify those most responsible for war crimes, crimes against humanity and other grave human rights violations), as well as the use of restorative justice, amnesties and the systems of incentives that lay behind these benefits. In a few words, "the more a *compareciente* (those investigated by the JEP) cooperates with the JEP by providing truth, acknowledging responsibility (if necessary), offering reparation and guaranteeing the non-recurrence of the crimes, the more lenient his or her sanction will be."

Keywords 2016 referendum · JEP's creation · Transitional justice judges · Transitional justice design · Colombian internal armed conflict · Transitional justice procedures · Colombian Peace Process · Special Jurisdiction for Peace · JEP

N. Zuluaga Afanador, *The Sociological Legitimacy of the Special Jurisdiction for Peace of Colombia*, St Antony's Series,
https://doi.org/10.1007/978-3-032-21912-1_3

In this chapter, I briefly describe the historical context of the JEP for the issues that might be relevant for the JEP's sociological legitimacy. I outline the JEP's origins, its design and the selection of the justices and their staff.

3.1 The JEP's Creation in Context

Throughout many decades, unaccountable acts of violence have struck Colombia—massacres, acts of sexual violence, kidnappings, torture and enforced disappearance, among others. Its effects have permeated collective consciousness and have entailed "a collective trauma that accumulates layers of experience, pain and resistance" (Truth Commision of Colombia 2022, 32). This trauma has been passing on from generation to generation in the form of memories and silence, and ends up consolidating "the identity of a country that has tried many times to build a peace that has resulted in fragmented processes and new cycles of violence" (Truth Commision of Colombia 2022, 32). In other words, the internal armed conflict has remarkably impacted the identity of Colombians and the lives of millions.

In 2023, it has been estimated that 9.7 million people have been victims in the context of the internal armed conflict (Unidad para la atención y reparación de las víctimas 2023). That means that roughly 1 out of 5 Colombians have suffered from victimisation and, certainly, the armed conflict between the Colombian State and the FARC-EP (1964–2016) deeply contributed to that process. The data of the crimes is revealing, as displayed in the Table 3.1.

Although the data in the table only account for some crimes, it is enough to understand the titanic challenge the Colombian State has faced to ensure the accountability of those crimes. As the armed conflict was

Table 3.1 Selection of crimes committed by the FARC-EP and State agents

	Total	*Percentage attributed to the FARC-EP*	*Percentage attributed to the State agents*
Homicides	450,000	21% (96,952)	12% (56,094)
Enforced disappearance	121,768	24% (29,410)	8% (9,359)
Kidnappings	50,770	40% (20,223)	X

Data Truth Commission of Colombia (2022)

happening, the ordinary courts investigated, adjudicated and punished many of these crimes on a case-by-case basis. Yet, their effectiveness was heavily criticised, and the rates of impunity were significantly high (Grupo de Memoria Histórica 2013, 197–99).

In June 2004, the Office of the ICC Prosecutor decided to open preliminary examinations for crimes against humanity and war crimes in the context of the armed conflict between guerrillas, paramilitaries and government forces.

In 2005, with the demobilisation of the AUC, a bill was passed to create a transitional justice judicial mechanism known as "Justice and Peace" / "Justicia y Paz". In this system, specialised prosecutors investigated crimes by both paramilitaries and organised armed groups who demobilised under these legal conditions. When judicial operators found grounds, they indicted individuals before specialised judges, who were included in the ordinary jurisdiction.

The results were somewhat discouraging. In the early years—from 2005 to 2011—most operation was based on a case-by-case basis. Only 8.8% of those who demobilised completed the process before the Office of the General Attorney. Moreover, in the first eight years, *Justicia y Paz* system only handed down ten convictions against fourteen defendants. These cases only recognised 2,856 victims—representing just 5.7% of the total number of victims linked to events confessed up to 2012 (Merchán Duque 2019, 37–38).

While acknowledging that Colombian authorities had carried out proceedings against different actors of the conflict, including individuals who might be considered most responsible for the crimes, the ICC Prosecutor observed in 2012 that "there remained a number of gaps or shortfalls which indicated insufficient or incomplete activity in relation to certain categories of persons and certain categories of crimes" (International Criminal Court 2024; International Criminal Court Office of the Prosecutor 2012).

Justicia y Paz's inefficacy in both ensuring victims' participation and securing effective convictions prompted a substantial reform. In 2012, a constitutional reform and new legislation transformed the system's investigation strategy by introducing a novel focus on "contextual analysis" (Merchán Duque 2019). This approach entailed establishing criteria for case prioritisation and selection, and promoted the adjudication of patterns of macro-level victimisation, rather than isolated events. While this shift improved efficiency, it also drew criticism, especially regarding victims' participation and guarantees for their rights.

In the context of the armed conflict with the FARC-EP, the JEP was designed to incorporate lessons learned from the *Justicia y Paz* process and from the victims' participation in the peace negotiations. Furthermore, it responded to two key imperatives.

First, it aimed to facilitate the Colombian transition, from an internal armed conflict to a more peaceful scenario, where democracy was strengthened and human rights were more guaranteed. Second, it ensured the accountability of war crimes and crimes against humanity, as a proof that the Colombian State was honouring the Statue of Rome's international obligations.

3.2 Main Elements of the JEP's Operation: Macro-cases, Restorative Justice, Incentives and Amnesties

Unlike the early stages of *Justicia y Paz* system, the JEP is a form of selective justice. It investigates patterns of criminalisation, identifying, trying and sanctioning only those most responsible[1] for war crimes, crimes against humanity and other grave human rights violations. To strengthen its operation, the JEP prioritises restorative justice over retributive justice providing a system of incentives. The more a *compareciente* cooperates with the JEP by providing truth, acknowledging responsibility—if necessary—offering reparation and guaranteeing the non-recurrence of the crimes, the more lenient his or her sanction will be.

For example, in the most cooperative scenario, those who are "most responsible" for the patterns of victimisation—kidnappings, "*falsos positivos*", among other crimes—might have a *sanción propia* or "proper sanction". This sanction consisted both a retributive element—between 5

[1] Although there has been debate around definition of the concept of "most responsible" both in the academia and in international courts (Michalowski et al. 2020, 12–14), for the purposes of this document, and paraphrasing Michalowski et al. (2020), the "most responsible" will be defined as the individual who had an essential role in the execution of the crimes, either as leader in a criminal structure or as a determinant participant in the design or formulation of a plan or policy of organized violence against civilian population.

and 8 years of restriction of liberty—and a restorative element—the imposition of restorative actions agreed with the victims, such as constructing roads or schools in the affected communities.

The restriction of liberty entails the confinement of the sentenced person to move within an area—probably no larger than a municipality—and it will not entail prison time. The exact details of this retributive component are not yet clear because the JEP competent authority, the Section of Acknowledgement of Responsibility and Truth (SeRVR in Spanish[2]), must establish them in the first *sanción propia* sentence, which has not been handed down as of May 2025.

In contrast, in the least cooperative scenario, the JEP might sentence a person to a *sanción ordinaria* "ordinary sanction", entailing between 15 and 20 years of imprisonment.

Furthermore, as selective justice, the JEP does not seek to adjudicate every crime on a case-by-case basis. Rather, it has opened 11 macro-cases to focus on representative cases, patterns of victimisation to figure out plans or policies of organised violence.

In them, the JEP's competent judicial authority, the Panel of Acknowledgement of Truth Responsibility (SRVR for its acronym in Spanish[3]) consolidates patterns of victimisation and identifies those who are most responsible for them after cross-checking sources coming from various actors. The origin of these sources is summarised in the acronym in Spanish VACE (victims, academia, *comparecientes* and *Estado*—State).

The SRVR communicates its findings through formal indictments directed at those deemed as most responsible for the crimes under investigation. In turn, the indicted individuals must decide whether they accept the indictment's charges and conditions indictment. As of May 2, 2025, the SRVR had handed down 16 indictments to 233 *comparecientes* in the macro-cases one, two, three, four, five and seven (Jurisdicción Especial para la Paz 2025g).[4]

[2] Sección de Primera Instancia para Casos de Reconocimiento de Verdad y Responsabilidad.

[3] Sala de Reconocimiento de Verdad y de Responsabilidad, y de Determinación de los Hechos y Conductas.

[4] On March 3, 2025, I submitted a Freedom of Information (FOI) request before the JEP, primarily asking about: (1) the number of cases where they had issued definitive rulings; (2) the status of the macro-cases; (3) the number of sanctions handed down; (4) the number of cases in trial. I received most information through a response on May 2,

If they acknowledge responsibility, the SRVR hears observations from the victims that have been recognised within the macro-cases, due to their direct interest in the legal studied subject. Later, the SRVR decides whether the terms of the acknowledgement satisfy the victims' rights.

If the SRVR find that the criteria are met, it convenes a restorative hearing between victims and *comparecientes*, known as the Hearing for the Acknowledgement of Responsibility and Truth (ARVR for its acronym in Spanish[5]). The preparation for the ARVR is thorough. JEP's psychosocial teams provide support to both victims and *comparecientes* through restorative processes—for instance, painting restored vases inspired by *Kintsugi* art, as previously described. Sometimes, private encounters between both victims and perpetrators are hold prior to the hearing, facilitating dialogue and emotional preparation. By May 2, 2025, the SRVR had conducted 8 ARVR within the macro-cases one, three and four. They were hold in several regions across Colombia—Bogotá, Cali, Huila, Antioquia, Casanare and Cesar (Jurisdicción Especial para la Paz 2025g).

Finally, in the ARVR, *comparecientes* confirm their responsibility for the crimes before the victims. Victims have the chance of facing the perpetrators and reacting to their statements. Justices act as mediators to foster dialogue and ensure the restorative operation of the event.

After the hearing, the SRVR mediates between both parties, so they agree on some of the restorative measures. Then the SRVR hands down "the resolution of conclusions", where it communicates its findings, the extent to which *comparecientes* acknowledged the truth and the proposed sanctions. As of March 31, 2025, it had issued four "resolutions of conclusions".

Once this procedure is finished, the case is transferred to a superior chamber—the First Instance Section of Acknowledgement of Responsibility and Truth. This Section verifies that the conditions of the acknowledgement are met, hears the victims and hands down a sentence that establishes the "proper sanctions" for those deemed as most responsible. By May 2, 2025, this Section had verified the acknowledgement of 19 *comparecientes,* issued a general strategy for dealing with victims'

2025, in the middle of a process to study my right to file such a FOI request. I had received an uncomplete response on March 26, 2025, and finally on May 20, 2025, the competent judicial authority within the JEP granted my right to request such information.

[5] In Spanish: "Audiencia de reconocimiento de verdad y responsabilidad".

participation (the ruling TP-SeRVR-APAS-CASA-No. 021-2023) and had begun conveying *comparecientes* and victims to agree on the restorative measures. However, as of May 2, 2025, this chamber had not handed down any "proper sanction"; it had not defined the legal situation of any most responsible perpetrator (Jurisdicción Especial para la Paz 2025g).

For those indicted who do not acknowledge their responsibility, the proceedings are different and are similar to a case in an ordinary court. After the *compareciente*'s refusal to accept the terms of the indictment, the SRVR sends the file to the Unit of Investigation and Accusation (UIA), the equivalent of the Attorney General's Office, which continues the investigation. In case it finds grounds, the competent prosecutor accuses the individual before a superior instance of the SRVR—the First Instance Section of Lack of Acknowledgement of Responsibility and Truth. Then, a trial similar to those of the ordinary jurisdiction begins. Prosecutors must prove before the Court that the indicted is guilty, who in turn either accepts the charges or defends themselves from the accusation. If the defendant is found guilty, they can have a sentence of 15–20 years in prison—*sanción ordinaria*, ("ordinary sanction"). If they acknowledge their culpability before the sentence, the sentence is from 5 to 8 years of prison—*sanción alternativa*, ("alternative sanction").

By May 2, 2025, the UIA had accused 5 individuals, all of them indicted for allegedly committing *falsos positivos.* The trial of one of them, Publio Hernán Mejía, had already started. It was at a stage of presenting evidence and eleven sessions had been already carried out (Jurisdicción Especial para la Paz 2025g).

Despite undeniable progress across various proceedings, it is important to stress the delays in handing down sanctions to those identified as most responsible. As the JEP itself has acknowledge: "As of today [May 2, 2025] none of the First Instance Sections of the Tribunal for Peace has imposed any proper, alternative, or ordinary sanctions" (Jurisdicción Especial para la Paz 2025g). As perceived in the interviews and media reports, this lack of enforcement has an impact on the JEP's legitimacy—an issue that will be further examined in Section 5.2.3.

3.3 Proceedings for Those Who Are Not Most Responsible for Patterns of Victimisation

The proceeding for those who are not most responsible for patterns of victimisation is designed to be shorter and initially adjudicated in two panels, depending on the type of crime. On the one hand, the Panel of Definition of Judicial Situations (SDSJ for its acronym in Spanish[6]) adjudicates the cases of those who allegedly committed serious human rights violations or breaks of international humanitarian law but are not considered as the most responsible for the crimes.

The Panel is responsible for verifying whether individuals comply with a regime of conditionalities, which requires them to fulfil duties regarding truth-telling, reparation and guarantees of non-recurrence for victims (Zuluaga Afanador 2021). The scale of the requirements is smaller than in most responsible cases, and compliance enables the Panel to close their case, which means that their judicial status is settled. This function is crucial because thousands of former members of the FARC-EP, agents of the State and civilians—all of whom either were under investigation or had been convicted in ordinary courts prior to the JEP's establishment—need clarification of their legal situation. As of May 2, 2025, the Panel had granted definitive legal benefits to 161 individuals: it waived the right to prosecute in 87 cases and declared the preclusion of the investigation in 74 cases. Moreover, it expelled 5 individuals from the JEP for not complying with the regime of conditionalities (Jurisdicción Especial para la Paz 2025g).

In the Colombian legal system, the crimes' pardon, or amnesties, only proceed for political crimes (e.g. rebellion—taking up arms against the State) or crimes directly related to political crimes (e.g. a theft exclusively conducted to finance the guerrilla group). Following the Peace Agreement and international standards set by the Article 6.5 of the Protocol II to the Geneva Conventions, the State should grant "the broadest possible amnesty" (Colombian Government and FARC-EP 2016). Consequently, just after the Peace Agreement was approved, between 2017 and March 2018, the Colombian Government and ordinary courts granted amnesties in 9,689 simple cases. However, many of those decisions were not communicated to around 9,600 of the beneficiaries at that time (Caracol Radio 2024). Just until February 2024, the JEP centralised that data so

[6] In Spanish: Sala de Definición de Situaciones Jurídicas.

that former members of the guerrilla had certainty of their situation (JEP Press Office 2024).

On the other hand, more complex cases of amnesties are adjudicated by the Panel of Amnesties and Pardons of the JEP. The Panel studies whether the connection of ordinary crimes to political crimes justifies the amnesty of the first. For example, they rule whether drug trafficking was related to financing the political cause of the guerrilla. The Panel studies such a connection and whether the case meets the criteria of international humanitarian law—proportionality, distinction, among others. In these cases, it has granted 976 amnesties, as of May 2, 2025 (Jurisdicción Especial para la Paz 2025g).

Understanding the JEP procedures is important because it contributes to assessing the sociopolitical implications of procedural decisions that move the process forward (e.g. "the resolution of conclusions") or final rulings that solve a person's judicial situation (e.g. ordinary, alternative or proper sanctions for those most responsible or decisions waiving the right to prosecute for those identified non-most responsible). Yet, as the JEP has not handed down any sentence as of May 2025, it is difficult to tell how those most responsible will be sanctioned and the impact of this decisions on public opinion.

In conclusion, the JEP's design only granted amnesty for political crimes and those related to it. Moreover, this design aimed at investigating, adjudicating and sanctioning serious human rights violations, by identifying those most responsible for these crimes due to their participation as key actors in the criminal system that perpetrated the patterns of violence. These individuals can acknowledge their responsibility in the crimes, cooperate with satisfying the victims' rights and receive more lenient sentences. Otherwise, they can defend their legal situation in an ordinary trial with the possibility of being convicted for up to 20 years.

Those deemed as non-most responsible should comply a system of conditions, contributing to satisfy the victims' rights. If these *comparecientes* honour these duties, they are granted definitive legal benefits, like the waiver of their investigations. When they fail to do so, they can be expelled from the JEP and their case is adjudicated in the ordinary justice with more severe sentences.

This design is different from the outcomes of "The Troubles" in Northern Ireland. According to Joseph Robinson, there has been little intervention to clarify the crimes committed during that conflict. In his own words, "more than 3,000 killings remain officially unsolved (indeed it would be safe to say there has been a de facto amnesty for all Troubles-related crimes since the signing of the Agreement), and there has been no serious or in-depth official truth recovery process" (Robinson 2017, 1). This difference in addressing human rights violations highlights the importance and ambition of the Colombian project of transitional justice.

3.4 The Selection and Progress in the Macro-cases and Their Relation to the Sociological Legitimacy of the JEP

The selection and progress of the macro-cases may describe how the JEP has progressively tried to satisfy different constituencies—victims of the FARC-EP, the Armed Forces, ethnic groups, women and LGBT+ communities. Furthermore, it also shows how the JEP has endeavoured to maintain equal treatment of the FARC-EP and the Armed Forces—there are three cases exclusively related to the FARC-EP, three related to the State forces or public authorities, and the five remaining cases involve both parties. Lastly, progress on the cases shows the JEP's speed in handing down definitive rulings, which might affect people's satisfaction with the JEP's operation.

As of May 2025, the SRVR, in charge of this function, had opened eleven macro-cases. It followed three criteria (Sala de Reconocimiento de Verdad y Responsabilidad 2018). First, the subjective criteria takes into account: (1) the victims' vulnerability condition (e.g. their gender and ethnic identity, their age, socio-economic conditions); (2) the differentiated impact on indigenous, gypsy, and afrodescendant peoples; (3) the damages on other groups, like peasants' communities, social leaders or union leaders; (4) and the potential participation of most responsible *comparecientes*.

Second, the objective standard considers the acts' seriousness, namely criminal acts that due to their duration, effects and *modus operandi* affect more seriously individual and collective fundamental rights in terms of intensity of violence, systematicity, massiveness and damages. Other objective considerations are: the magnitude of the victimisation in terms of number of victims, duration in time of the victimising events and extension in the territory; and the representativeness of the victimising events, understood as the quality of illustrating the *modus operandi* of criminal patterns under the JEP's jurisdiction. Finally, the complementary criteria concern the availability of data and logistic resources and feasibility of the access to information.

Most of the macro-cases involve the most common and atrocious crimes committed during the internal armed conflict: enforced disappearance, kidnapping, torture, sexual violence, homicides, illegal use of landmines, enforced recruitment, forced displacement, illegal attacks against the civil population, and illegal attacks against the environment and the territory, among others.

Among the macro-cases there are three types. First, national, regarding one type of crime or several crimes committed at a national level.

Second, territorial, concerning the study of crimes under the jurisdiction of the JEP in a specific area that was heavily victimised. Due to the strong connection to the territory, the territorial cases usually involve the participation of "*resguardos indígenas*", or indigenous territories in English, which are autonomous, independent, indigenous entities that rule their ancestral territory, and "*consejos comunitarios*", or community councils, similar institutions for afro descendants.

Third, umbrella cases are macro-cases that pertain to one actor and its relations with crimes that are not included in the national or territorial macro-cases. Below is a Table 3.2 that summarises the current macro-cases and their status.

As Table 3.2 shows, most of the cases are in the early stages, either in preparation, in interviews or in the stage of the victims' comments to the comparecientes' interviews. The cases that have progressed the furthest are one and three, where many *comparecientes* are on trial after duly acknowledging their responsibilities. Among them, there are the seven surviving members of the last Secretariat—the highest body of military command of the former FARC-EP—and two generals of the Army.

As of May 2, 2025, the JEP had indicted 233 *comparecientes* as "most responsible" for war crimes and crimes against humanity. Only 15 refused to accept the JEP's indictment. They are being investigated by the UIA and, if necessary, accused before the competent JEP Court (JEP Press Office 2023).

Table 3.2 Macro-cases of the JEP

Case	*1*	*2*	*3*
Name	Taking of hostages and other serious deprivations of freedom	Tumaco, Ricaurte and Barbacoas	Falsos positivos
Opening date	July 4, 2018	July 10, 2018	July 17, 2018
Level	National	Territorial	National
Actor(s)	FARC-EP	FARC-EP and Armed Forces	Armed Forces
Facts investigated	Kidnappings and other crimes committed in the context of the kidnappings between 1993 and 2012	War crimes and crimes against humanity perpetrated against peasants, members of the LGBT+ community, afrodescendants, indigenous people and their territories in the municipalities of Tumaco, Ricaurte and Barbacoas, in Nariño, southwest Colombia	Extrajudicial killings and enforced disappearances presented as casualties amid combats

Case	*1*	*2*	*3*
Number of victims	21,396 fully identified victims of kidnapping	No data	6,402
Stage	7 former members of the Secretariat, the highest body of military command of the former FARC-EP, are being trailed by the Section for cases of Acknowledgement of Responsibility The SRVR has indicted all those identified as most responsible for every of the seven Blocs, regional FARC-EP organisations Members of two of these Blocs have already acknowledged their responsibility in two hearings *(Comando Conjunto Central, Bloque Occidental)*	15 former members of the FARC-EP have been indicted	Three "resolutions of conclusions" have been issued 176 people have been indicted for crimes committed in Antioquia, Huila, Casanare, Norte de Santander, Caribbean Area and Catatumbo Ongoing investigation at a national level and in other regions Several members of the Armed Forces are on trial for the cases of Catatumbo, Casanare, after accepting their responsibility in the macro-patterns of victimisation Five have been accused by the UIA. One of them is on trial
Victims accredited by the JEP	4,151	105,241 individuals. Most of them are members of 30 community councils, 84 indigenous territories and organisations of peasants and six organisations of victims	4,222

(continued)

Table 3.2 (continued)

Case	*4*	*5*	*6*	*7*
Name	Urabá	North of Cauca and South of Valle del Cauca	Unión Patriótica Political Party	Forced recruitment and use of children
Opening date	September 11, 2018	November 16, 2018	February 26, 2019	March 1, 2019
Level	Territorial	Territorial	National	National
Actor(s)	Armed forces, FARC-EP, 9 civilians involved voluntarily	FARC-EP, Armed Forces	Armed Forces and Intelligence Forces	FARC-EP
Facts investigated	Serious human rights violations and breaches of the International Humanitarian Law in the Urabá region, northwest Colombia Studies two periods: 1986–2002 and 2002–2016	Grave human rights violations and breaches of the International Humanitarian Law in the region between the North of Cauca and South of Valle del Cauca, southwest Colombia. The studied period is between 1993 and 2016	Crimes against members of that party motivated by the membership of the victim to that party, a party created in the midst of the negotiations between the FARC and the Government in 1985	Forced recruitment and use of children committed by the FARC-EP, between 1996 and 2016
Number of victims	No data	365,967 identified victims across four regions of the country	Between 1984 and 2016: 4,616 victims of homicide 1,117 victims of enforced disappearance 2,217 victims of forced displacement	18,677 victims
Stage	Victims' comments to the *comparecientes*' interviews Ten people indicted in coordination with the macro-case three One ARVR conducted	Indictment to 22 members of two former FARC-EP armed structures Indictment to the other structures pending and to the individuals of Armed Forces	Victims' comments to the *comparecientes*' interviews	Six former members of the FARC-EP Secretariat have been indicted

Case	*4*	*5*	*6*	*7*
Victims accredited by the JEP	48,999	Several organisations have been recognised as victims: 129 collective entities—45 indigenous peoples, 67 communitarian councils and 8 victims' organisations. These entities represent more than 180,000 victims	297 victims. Among them, four are collective: the Partido Unión Patriótica (UP), the Colombian Communist Party, the Union Sintramienergética, and the organisation Central Nacional Provivienda (CENAPROV)	10,065 (8,903 of them are members of indigenous peoples)

Case	*8*	*9*	*10*	*11*
Name	Crimes committed by the Armed Forces and the paramilitaries	Crimes against ethnic peoples and their territories	Non-amnistiable crimes committed by the FARC-EP	Sexual violence
Opening date	August 30, 2022	September 13, 2022	July 15, 2022	September 27, 2023
Level	Umbrella	Umbrella	Umbrella	National
Actor	Armed Forces, Third parties	FARC-EP, Armed Forces	FARC-EP	FARC-EP, Armed Forces
Facts investigated	Serious human rights violations and breaches of international humanitarian law committed by the Armed Forces with participation of paramilitaries, other agents of the State and civilians	Crimes perpetrated by the FARC-EP or the Armed Forces, with the participation of paramilitaries or civilians against ethnic peoples and their territories	Non-amnistiable crimes committed by the FARC-EP	Sexual violence committed by the former FARC-EP or the Armed Forces

(continued)

Table 3.2 (continued)

Case	*8*	*9*	*10*	*11*
Number of victims	Provisional Universe of victims: 72,492	1,350,181 Provisional universe of victims with ethnic origin. 365,967 identified victims in four regions of the country	Provisional universe: 54,000 victims of forced displacement 50,100 victims of the illicit use of means of war, among them illegal land mines and explosives, attacks to protected individuals by International Humanitarian Law 48,000 victims of homicide 15,000 victims of enforced disappearance	35,178 victims of all the armed actors between 1957 and 2016.
Stage	Interviews to the *comparecientes*	Interviews to the *comparecientes*	Interviews to the *comparecientes*	Documenting information about the victims
Victims accredited by the JEP	No available data	No available data	169,400: probable universe of the victims who would be interested in participating in the process	No available data

Source Jurisdicción Especial para la Paz (2025a, b, c, d, e, f, g) and JEP Government Board (2024). Access date: June, 2, 2025

3.5 The Selection of the Justices, Their Staff and Their Effects on the JEP's Operation and Sociological Legitimacy

The process of selection of the JEP's justices is related to the JEP's sociological legitimacy in that its transparency and representativeness may have fostered trust. But it also has prompted the *Uribismo*, namely Álvaro Uribe Vélez, his supporters and their party CD, to criticise that the justices are biased: allegedly they would have a leftist ideology and their connections with social organisations would prevent them from being impartial (Semana 2021, 2023).

The academic background of many of the justices in critic legal theories and their conceptions of the Law may also make them more prone to leave behind a formalistic positivist approach and make risky and innovative decisions, compared to traditional lawyers or judges who tend to have more formalist approaches to Law. These factors have influenced the accountability of human rights in other contexts, as González-Ocantos has thoroughly explained for the cases of Argentina, Perú and México (2017).

The JEP justices were selected by a varied and independent Committee in a transparent process. The Committee was composed of delegates of the Supreme Court, the UN General Secretary, the Commission of the Colombian Universities, the Presidency of the European Court of Human Rights and the International Center of Transitional Justice. Similarly, the justices had to meet certain criteria of representation. According to Santiago Pardo-Rodríguez, who conducted a mixed methods study on the selection process, the Selection Committee fostered transparency by using a digital mechanism that used an algorithm, allowing public comments about the candidates that could alert the Committee of hidden conflicts of interest, and holding public interviews (2020). Thus, on September 26, 2017, the Committee chose a varied spectrum of justices. It prioritised lawyers who were not born in Bogotá, women, Afro-Colombians and indigenous people. For the first time in the history of Colombia, most of the justices were women (28 out of 51 appointed justices), and 20% were indigenous or afro descendants (Pardo Rodriguez 2020).

Apart from the selection of the justices, the appointment and administrative design of the staff have impacted the JEP's operation. It has made it difficult to effectively deal with backlogs in the Panels, hence, slowing the JEP's operations. In the first years of the JEP, most of the work was done by the Panels, whose personnel was lower in number and had less education and professional experience.

Thus, one of the first relevant issues that the JEP had to face was the staff—how many officers should every department in the JEP have? Who appoints them? How do the justices distribute the workforce in correspondence with the workload? Allegedly, Néstor Raul Correa, the JEP's executive secretary, was proposing that the members of staff would constitute a common group that could be flexibly allocated to the justices according to their needs, as the Inter-American Court of Human Rights works.

In contrast, some of the justices were more inclined to adopt a system similar to the one Colombian High Courts have, where every justice has an office with many officers that are appointed directly by him or her. In the end, the JEP opted for the second option (Uprimny 2018; Liévano 2024).

As a result, justices appointed the members of their offices, and the three Panels had less staff and staff of a lower hierarchy than the Sections, their superiors. However, so far, the Panels have had the great bulk of the JEP's workload, and they could not delegate some of their functions to their staff such as conducting interviews because they did not have the necessary rank to do so.

In fact, until the first "*resolución de conclusiones*", where the SRVR sent the first cases to the Sections, the Sections' staff had little work to do regarding their functions. To solve this problem, the justices used the mechanism of "mobility", whereby a justice and their whole office or particular officers are mobilised, or temporarily transferred, to other Sections or Panels that have a backlog of cases. A downside of this mechanism is that those transfers were not decided collectively by a higher authority, but they relied ultimately on the will of the justice, and sometimes they only entailed the occupation of a portion of their working hours, as an interviewee from the JEP commented.[7]

In the first years of operation, the Panels faced most of the workload of the JEP and had to figure out the process of operation of their functions, with less personnel than the other sections, and without the possibility

[7] Interviewee 11, interview by author, Bogotá, 08/30/2023. From now on, the interviewees who only agreed to participate anonymously will be identified with a number. Otherwise, if they agreed that they would be identifiable, I will use their name, following their consent forms.

of asking for an increase in personnel due to the adverse political environment during Duque's administration. This could partly explain the progress delays of the macro-cases. As I will later explain, this has an effect on the JEP's legitimacy: the slow pace of its functioning has frustrated the victims' expectations and even those of the former FARC-EP, undermining trust in the institution and challenging its effectiveness. Being a technical and niche issue, the reasons of that slow outcome are unknown to the majority of Colombians.

After Gustavo Petro, from the *Pacto Histórico* or Historical Pact coalition, was elected President in 2022, the JEP received approval to increase its personnel. And it has done so, creating more posts for "*magistrados auxiliares*", or auxiliary judges, the highest rank below a justice. This is expected to speed up the processes. Yet, the appointment process was not transparent and it is not clear that it is the most effective to clear the backlog of the Panels.

Unlike the original selection process of the justices, the process of selecting 36 auxiliary judges was not public, nor was the selection criteria. Candidates did not hear from their applications or interviews, and most of the appointed professionals were already working in the institution (Liévano 2024; Paola Molano Ayala [@pmolanoayala] 2024). Paola Molano, coordinator of the Transitional Justice area at the think-thank Dejusticia, criticised that the JEP did not argue why they opted to allocate the resources to the highest rank of lawyers, instead of hiring more lower-rank professionals. These processes might undermine the JEP's transparency and trustworthiness.

References

Caracol Radio. 2024. "Así se perdieron 9 decretos con las amnistías para 9.600 exFarc." Caracol Radio, May 6. https://caracol.com.co/2024/05/06/asi-se-perdieron-9-decretos-con-las-amnistias-para-9600-exfarc/.

Colombian Government and FARC-EP. 2016. "Peace Agreement 2016." November 26. https://www.peaceagreements.org/wview/1845/Final%20Agreement%20to%20End%20the%20Armed%20Conflict%20and%20Build%20a%20Stable%20and%20Lasting%20Peace.

González Ocantos, Ezequiel. 2017. *Shifting Legal Visions: Judicial Change and Human Rights Trials in Latin America*. Cambridge University Press. https://www.cambridge.org/core/books/shifting-legal-visions/CC9D850D90D984A72AA455DC32A8C56D.

Grupo de Memoria Histórica. 2013. *¡Basta ya! Colombia, memorias de guerra y dignidad: informe general*. Segunda edición corregida. Centro Nacional de Memoria Histórica.

International Criminal Court. 2024. "Colombia | International Criminal Court." May 13. https://www.icc-cpi.int/colombia.

International Criminal Court Office of the Prosecutor. 2012. *Situation in Colombia - Interim Report*. ICC Office of the Prosecutor. https://www.icc-cpi.int/sites/default/files/2022-09/OTPCOLOMBIAPublicInterimReportNovember2012.pdf.

JEP Government Board. 2024. "Acuerdo 7 de 2024." February 16. https://www.jep.gov.co/organosgobierno/Acuerdo%20AOG%20007%20de%202024.pdf.

JEP Press Office. 2023. "JEP ha imputado a 148 máximos responsables de crímenes de guerra y lesa humanidad en el conflicto armado." December 5. https://www.jep.gov.co:443/Sala-de-Prensa/Paginas/-jep-ha-imputado-a-148-maximos-responsables-de-crimenes-de-guerra-y-lesa-humanidad-en-el-conflicto-armado.aspx.

JEP Press Office. 2024. "JEP comunica decretos de amnistía a más de 9.600 firmantes del Acuerdo Final de Paz." February 21. https://www.jep.gov.co:443/Sala-de-Prensa/Paginas/-jep-comunica-decretos-de-amnistia-a-mas-de-9600-firmantes-del-acuerdo-final-de-paz.aspx.

Jurisdicción Especial para la Paz. 2025a. "Caso 01: Toma de rehenes, graves privaciones de la libertad y otros crímenes concurrentes cometidos por las Farc-EP." June 2. https://www.jep.gov.co/macrocasos/caso01.html.

Jurisdicción Especial para la Paz. 2025b. "Caso 03: Asesinatos y desapariciones forzadas presentados como bajas en combate por agentes del Estado." June 2. https://www.jep.gov.co/macrocasos/caso03.html.

Jurisdicción Especial para la Paz. 2025c. "Caso 04: Situación territorial de la región de Urabá." June 2. https://www.jep.gov.co/macrocasos/caso04.html.

Jurisdicción Especial para la Paz. 2025d. "Caso 09: Crímenes no amnistiables cometidos contra Pueblos y Territorios Étnicos en el marco del conflicto armado colombiano." June 2. https://www.jep.gov.co/macrocasos/caso09.html.

Jurisdicción Especial para la Paz. 2025e. "Caso 10: Crímenes no amnistiables cometidos por las extintas Farc-EP en el marco del conflicto armado colombiano." June 2. https://www.jep.gov.co/macrocasos/caso10.html.

Jurisdicción Especial para la Paz. 2025f. "Caso 11: Violencia basada en género, violencia sexual, violencia reproductiva, y otros crímenes cometidos por prejuicio basados en la orientación sexual, la expresión y/o identidad de género diversa en el marco del conflicto armado colombiano." June 2. https://www.jep.gov.co/macrocasos/caso11.html.

Jurisdicción Especial para la Paz. 2025g. "Response to Freedom of Information Request." Jurisdicción Especial para la Paz, May 2.

Liévano, Andrés Bermúdez. 2024. "El pecado original interno de la JEP de Colombia." *JusticeInfo.net*, March 1. https://www.justiceinfo.net/es/129032-el-pecado-original-interno-de-la-jep-de-colombia.html.

Merchán Duque, Mateo. 2019. "Historia Del Proceso de Configuración Normativa de La Herramienta de 'Contexto' En El Sistema de Justicia y Paz: La Tensión Entre La Legitimidad Para Las Víctimas y La Eficiencia Del Sistema." Pontificia Universidad Javeriana. http://hdl.handle.net/10554/45216 La - Spanish.

Michalowski, Sabine, Michael Cruz Rodríguez, and Hobeth Martínez Carrillo. 2020. *¿A quiénes sancionar? máximos responsables y participación determinante en la Jurisdicción Especial para la Paz*. Documentos Dejusticia 61. Dejusticia.

Paola Molano Ayala [@pmolanoayala]. 2024. "La decisión de la @JEP_Colombia de nombrar 36 magistrados auxiliares parece escandalosa, teniendo en cuenta que, con arandelas, son salarios de 37 millones de pesos. Además de esto, la decisión da lugar a, al menos, dos discusiones 🧵." Tweet. Twitter, February 5. https://twitter.com/pmolanoayala/status/1754328356038857146.

Pardo Rodriguez, Santiago. 2020. "A Second Chance on Earth: Understanding the Selection Process of the Judges of the Colombian Special Jurisdiction for Peace." *Notre Dame Journal of International & Comparative Law* 10: 209.

Robinson, Joseph S. 2017. *Transitional Justice and the Politics of Inscription: Memory, Space and Narrative in Northern Ireland*. 1st ed. Routledge. https://doi.org/10.4324/9781315265308.

Sala de Reconocimiento de Verdad y Responsabilidad. 2018. *Criterios y Metodología de Priorización de Casos y Situaciones*. Jurisdicción Especial para la Paz. https://www.jep.gov.co/documents/criteriosymetodologiadepriorizacion.pdf.

Semana. 2021. "'No es magistrado sino politiquero que aumenta la ilegitimidad de la JEP': Uribe critica a Eduardo Cifuentes." Semana.com Últimas Noticias de Colombia y el Mundo, August 30. https://www.semana.com/nacion/articulo/no-es-magistrado-sino-politiquero-que-aumenta-la-ilegitimidad-de-la-jep-uribe-critica-a-eduardo-cifuentes/202145/.

Semana. 2023. "Expresidente Uribe revela denuncia en la que le aseguran que la magistrada de la JEP Caterina Heyck está 'obsesionada' con él." Semana.com Últimas Noticias de Colombia y el Mundo, November 19. https://www.semana.com/politica/articulo/expresidente-uribe-revela-denuncia-en-la-que-le-aseguran-que-la-magistrada-de-la-jep-caterina-heyck-esta-obsesionada-con-el/202334/.

Truth Commision of Colombia. 2022. *Hallazgos y recomendaciones: de la Comisión de la Verdad de Colombia*. Primera edición. Hay futuro si hay verdad, Tomo 2,3. Comisión de la Verdad.

Unidad para la atención y reparación de las víctimas. 2023. "Registro Único de Víctimas (RUV)." Registro Único de Víctimas, February 28. https://www.unidadvictimas.gov.co/es/registro-unico-de-victimas-ruv/37394.

Uprimny, Rodrigo. 2018. "¿Cuál estructura para la JEP?" *Dejusticia*, January 21. https://www.dejusticia.org/column/cual-estructura-para-la-jep/.

Zuluaga Afanador, Nicolás. 2021. *El Cumplimiento Colectivo Del Deber de Reparación En La Jurisdicción Especial Para La Paz Desafíos y Aprendizajes Para Agilizar El Procesamiento Del Régimen de Condicionalidad*. ETJN Working Papers Series. https://repository.essex.ac.uk/31780/1/ETJN_DT3_Cumplimiento%20colectivo_new_logo.pdf.

CHAPTER 4

Conceptual Framework

Abstract This chapter clarifies the conceptual framework of the book. Firstly, it provides an explanation of the JEP's legitimacy. Drawing on the relevant academic literature, notably David Beetham's and Cohen et al.'s definition, I opted for a sociological definition as "the right a judicial institution has to make judicial decisions, according to some social perceptions and beliefs". In my own words, "a legitimate court has a right to rule not in terms of governing a territory or a society, but in the sense that it has the social authority to hand down decisions, opinions, and judgements 'which those normatively addressed must obey, or at least consider with due care' (Cohen et al. 2018, 4)". Building on an understanding that legitimacy varies over time, I identified the key factors that affect legitimacy, proposed a way of operationalising them and assessed their current levels. As a result, I summarised from the literature five key factors: (1) diffuse support; (2) specific support; (3) obedience; (4) salience; and (5) the age of the institution. In the several subsections, I explained each one of them.

Keywords Sociological legitimacy · Diffuse support · Specific support · Obedience · Salience · Measurement of legitimacy · Normative legitimacy · Legitimacy of Courts · Legitimacy of transitional justice mechanisms

N. Zuluaga Afanador, *The Sociological Legitimacy of the Special Jurisdiction for Peace of Colombia*, St Antony's Series,
https://doi.org/10.1007/978-3-032-21912-1_4

Assessing and explaining the legitimacy of the JEP is definitively a complex task. To my knowledge, academic literature has not specifically studied the legitimacy of a transitional justice judicial mechanism, and Gibson and Caldeira, the authors that have broadly studied the high court's legitimacy, do not provide a straightforward definition of the concept. Moreover, scholars have not developed a method for operationalising this concept and the factors that influence this dependent variable. In this chapter, I attempt to fill that gap in the literature.

Drawing on the existing literature, I begin by defining the legitimacy of a transitional justice tribunal and select the factors that strengthen or erode such legitimacy. I then operationalise such factors by proposing some measures that would indicate the extent those factors work in the case of the JEP. Finally, I gauge those measures on a scale that describes the degree of the JEP's legitimacy in Colombian society.

4.1 The Concept of Legitimacy in the JEP's Context

Etymologically, the word "legitimacy" comes from lex (law) and timus (belonging to), so it originally means "belonging to the law" (Pianigiani 1907). This primary definition shows that the term "legitimacy" is closely related to the law.

In the introduction of his seminal work "Legitimation of Power", David Beetham considers this legal approach as one of the three approaches that explain the legitimacy of power—along with a moral philosophy and a social sciences approach. Although this book is about the legitimacy of transitional justice courts, Beetham's explanations of the legitimacy of power are also applicable. In the end, transitional courts also exert their power to adjudicate crimes committed during armed conflicts.

According to Beetham, lawyers, and especially constitutional experts, focus on the resolution of legal disputes about power—they resolve issues like who is authorised to exercise power?, what are the limits to it?, and how this authorisation is acquired? These actors are concerned about the definition and interpretation of legal rules and its inception, revision and enforcement. In Beetham's words: "For them, power is legitimate where its acquisition and exercise conform to established law. For them legitimacy is equivalent to legal validity" (Beetham 2002, 4). This notion is commonly known as normative legitimacy.

In contrast, moral and political philosophers have usually been curious about whether the rules that are used to exert power are justifiable following "rationally defensible normative principles" (Beetham 2002, 5). The main issue of legitimacy is not what the law prescribes, but rather what the law ought to prescribe. These authors make a universal claim that defensible principles do not belong to a specific society, but they are shared by any rational person—"what is 'legitimate to the philosopher', then, is what is morally justifiable or rightful" (Beetham 2002, 5).

In turn, social scientists, like Beetham, are more concerned with studying the empirical implications of legitimacy on the characteristics of power relations—e.g. the level of obedience or support those in power can expect from their subordinates. Understanding legitimacy contributes to describe why people have different expectations from power relationships, why institutions operate differently across societies, and why there is more coercion in some contexts than in others. Notably, it is useful to explain the erosion of power relations and breaches in social and political orders. Following Weber, these thinkers argue that what matters is what a society believes, rather than what an individual thinks. Legitimacy is "the belief in legitimacy on the part of the relevant social agents; and power relations [are] legitimate where those involved in them, subordinate as well as dominant, believe them to be so" (Beetham 2002, 6).

Unlike Beetham, I will not follow a single approach. I will take into account both the moral and the social scientist approach because it is more suitable for understanding the controversies around the JEP's legitimacy. First, the JEP already has normative legitimacy, but its operation is still contested. The JEP has normative legitimacy because a set of laws recognises its existence, regulates its procedures and was approved by more demanding procedures in Congress, which means they had reinforced political support.[1] Furthermore, the Constitutional Court, which reviews the constitutionality of laws and amendments, reviewed the creation of the JEP and the Statutory Law and ruled that they were constitutional, although it made some adjustments. For instance,

[1] In total, there is one amendment to the Constitution and two Laws regulating the JEP: the Legislative Act 01 of 2017 (a constitutional amendment approved by Congress that creates the JEP); the Statutory Law 1957 of 2019 (that rules the JEP operation); and the Law of Procedures 1922 of 2019. The first two types of laws require more demanding processes to get approved. Thus, the success in passing those bills means that they achieved reinforced political approval in Congress.

the Constitutional Court ruled that civilians, be they public servants or not, should not be forced to be investigated by the JEP, but rather by their natural judge: the ordinary jurisdiction. Thus, a robust set of laws reviewed by the Constitutional Court regulates the JEP, which has been operating within that legal framework.

Second, controversies around the JEP involve both the moral justification of the law—is restorative justice proportionate and fair to adjudicate grave human rights violations?—and the implications of legitimacy on power relations—if society does not perceive JEP's operation as legitimate, can this institution accomplish its objectives? Is it sustainable over time? As a result, I seek to explore the term "legitimacy" beyond a legal aspect, and I use a sociological definition, which combines both approaches, to verify whether the Colombian society acknowledges the legal authority of the JEP. Thus, I will define legitimacy as "the right a judicial institution has to make judicial decisions, according to social perceptions and beliefs".

This definition draws on Cohen et al.'s definition (2018, 4). They claimed that a legitimate power is "one that has 'the right to rule'". Thus, a legitimate court has a right to rule not in terms of governing a territory or a society, but in the sense that it has the social authority to hand down decisions, opinions and judgements "which those normatively addressed must obey, or at least consider with due care" (Cohen et al. 2018, 4).

One implication of that definition is that individuals acknowledge social authority to the judicial institution itself, aside from valuing its decisions. Although this will be better explained below, it constitutes the separation between diffuse support (a social group's loyalty to the judicial institution) and specific support (how satisfied a social group is regarding particular decisions).

Another implication is that to understand the legitimacy of a judicial institution, one must analyse whether the beliefs and values of a social group are consistent with its perception of the institution. Thus, the image of the institution, the symbols it uses (robes, language, setting of the press conferences, colours) and the exposure of the social group to these symbols are essential to understand its legitimacy (Gibson et al. 1998). Specially, the framing of the decisions is very important (Forero-Alba and Rodríguez-Raga 2022), namely the rulings' writing style, the case's description and the communication of the decisions, in other words, the practices involved in hearings and rulings.

In particular, when it comes to the JEP's legitimacy, the values in question are primarily justice and peace. For a social group, the value of justice might be that the JEP should properly adjudicate and sanction the crimes committed during the internal armed conflict with the FARC-EP, while also guaranteeing the victims' rights to truth, reparation and non-repetition. However, the tension that compromises legitimacy is consolidated when opposing beliefs clash. On the one hand, a social group might believe that the only way to have justice is by imprisoning someone responsible for their actions (Gomez-Suarez 2016). On the other hand, the JEP symbolises a belief that prioritises restorative justice by incentivising the dialogue between perpetrators and victims to find common ground in terms of truth and reparations. These connections are favoured by offering legal benefits to *comparecientes* in exchange for their cooperation in fulfilling the victims' rights (truth, reparation, guarantees of non-recurrence and justice). Furthermore, these actions aim to reconstruct social relationships and restore the victim's dignity, leaving imprisonment in second place.

In terms of peace, there are also contrasting beliefs. A social group may think that peace should be attained when the good defeats the bad; in other words, when the State, defending the People, defeats the terrorists of the FARC. An alternative vision may be that there are no winners and that the Peace Agreement was signed not only to end the war but also to overcome the structural flaws in the State construction process that facilitated the internal armed conflict.

By the time peace conversations started in 2012, several years of armed confrontation had led to what Zartman would call "mutually hurting stalemate" (2001), a deadlock where both parties have few choices and yet are assuming significant losses (Santos 2019; De la Calle Lombana 2019). The FARC-EP could hardly overthrow the Government. They did not have enough military power and social support. Conversely, the Government could hardly defeat the guerrilla without putting the lives of thousands at risk and allocating limited resources to strengthen the Armed Forces. This situation convinced both parties to start peace conversations.

Furthermore, the Peace Agreement aimed to stop the direct armed confrontation, achieving negative peace—or the absence of personal violence. It also has several provisions to prevent the causes of the conflict—or fostering positive peace, overcoming structural violence, as Galtung posited (Galtung 1969, 51, 52). In fact, the points one, two and four of the Peace Agreement aim to improve rural conditions through territorial development plans, increase land distribution, foster political representation and implement several measures to tackle drug production, among other specifications. The first belief might be represented in Álvaro Uribe's critiques and the latter in the JEP.

This brief discussion on the different beliefs on peace and justice partially describes why I opted for a sociological definition of legitimacy, rather than legal. Most of the initial and consistent critiques of the JEP are moral. The campaign of the NO in the plebiscite emphasised that the JEP would mean impunity because the top commanders of the FARC-EP would not pay for their crimes and would end up serving as congressmen (Gomez-Suarez 2016). This can be summarised in banners of the campaigners against the 2016 Peace Agreement that said "No Impunity / No FARC in Congress" (El Espectador 2020).

In the JEP's early years and as of 2024, many public figures have criticised the JEP, arguing incompatibilities with their conceptions of justice, peace and impartiality, rather than disagreeing on legal grounds. For instance, former Presidents Álvaro Uribe Vélez and Iván Duque, Paloma Valencia, a prestigious congresswoman of their party, and the journalist Maria Isabel Rueda argued that the JEP was designed to guarantee impunity to the FARC (Gómez 2022; Valencia Valencia and Francés-Gómez 2018).

In summary, I opted to study the JEP's sociological legitimacy because the most frequent and strong critiques against the JEP come from the lack of correspondence between the values it represents and those from critical social sectors. Furthermore, the vast set of laws, sentences and signs of international support indicate that the JEP has legal and somewhat political legitimacy. Now that legitimacy has been defined and contextualised to the JEP's case, it is essential to operationalise it and explain how to measure it for the JEP.

4.2 Operationalisation of the Concept of Legitimacy

Every judicial institution has a legitimacy capital that varies over time (Cohen et al. 2018, 5; Lupu 2013, 443). According to Cohen et al. (2018, 5), legitimacy can also be internal or external. It might address the opinions of the insiders—those who work within the institutionally studied regime, like the clerks of the JEP, the victims' attorneys who participate in its operation, or the victims who are accredited—or it might concern the insights of the outsiders, of people beyond the institution. This study combines both views: it uses sources from insiders and outsiders to describe different perceptions of the JEP.

Apart from the internal and external perspectives, this book probes into the factors that might affect the JEP's legitimacy capital over time. I collected them after reviewing relevant literature about the legitimacy of judicial institutions, especially Gibson et al. (1998), Gibson and Caldeira (2003, 9), Easton (1975), Shany (2014), and Botero (2020). In total, I identified five factors, and I operationalised them to study how they strengthened or eroded the JEP's legitimacy. The five factors are: diffuse support, specific support, salience, obedience and the age of the institution. In the following sections, I will explain every factor. Then, in a table, I will propose signs that may show how a judicial institution's legitimacy is strengthening or eroding.

4.2.1 *Diffuse and Specific Support*

According to Botero (2020), who draws on Gibson and Caldeira (2003, 9) and Easton's work (1975), diffuse support is strongly associated with loyalty (even a loyal opposition), whereas specific support means the individuals' satisfaction with particular judicial decisions. When individuals are loyal to a judicial institution, they defend it, even when the judicial authority makes decisions they disagree with. In other words, theoretically diffuse support and specific support are independent variables from each other.

Over time, and by pleasing diverse constituencies, judicial institutions build a goodwill reservoir. This allows them to offset any negative reactions in future. Thus, diffuse support can be measured through the sociopolitical willingness to adopt fundamental changes to the institution, support from other institutions to reinforce the JEP's operation or protect it, the willingness of individuals to accept contentious decisions, and signs of loyalty and favourable opinion towards the institution.

As for specific support, it can depend on the extent to which the decision corresponds to the individual's beliefs and values, as was argued before. Yet, there is another aspect that is equally essential: framing. Framing is "the process by which a communication source [...] defines and constructs a political issue or public controversy" (Nelson et al. 1997,

567). This is essentially what judges do. By deciding on a public controversy, regardless of the scale, and by communicating the construction they made, they frame an issue.

Consistent academic literature has pointed out that individuals are keener to support judicial decisions that are based on "scientific and legal" reasons, rather than on political reasons (Forero-Alba and Rodríguez-Raga 2022; Voeten 2013; Gibson et al. 1998, 345). In fact, judges can frame unpopular decisions, so they seem as if they are the outcome of a legal obligation or system, rather than the result of a political decision. As Gibson et al. have stated: "Courts garner legitimacy from pleasing decisions but lose little or nothing from displeasing decisions, since they can transfer responsibility for unpopular decisions to the 'law'" (Gibson et al. 1998, 354). Specifically, Forero-Alba and Rodríguez-Raga have stressed that the Colombian Constitutional Court translates specific support into diffuse support by successfully framing its rulings to convey a sense of neutrality, reasoning and impartiality. In that framing process, scientific arguments are more effective than any other arguments, including normative ones (2022, 190).

In terms of operationalisation, specific support can be observed in the victims' satisfaction in salient JEP cases, in the number of victims participating in the JEP's proceedings, delays in handing down final rulings, the type of framing used in the decisions and their communication, the perceived satisfaction in different social groups, and the equal treatment in investigating, adjudicating and sanctioning FARC-EP and Armed Forces members. By carrying out the interviews during fieldwork, I was able to identify that the satisfaction of different social groups might also be affected by whether the JEP equally investigates the FARC-EP and the Armed Forces, as well as the speed in handing down decisions.

4.2.2 *Salience*

The salience of the judicial institution is the extent to which people understand how the institution operates, what its symbols are (robes, hearings, seals), and what its functions are. In terms of legitimacy, salience is important in that "to know courts is to love them, because to know them is to be exposed to a series of legitimizing messages focused on the symbols of justice, judicial objectivity, and impartiality" (Gibson et al. 1998, 345). Thus, people who know how high courts operate are more exposed to the mythology that Courts decide using legal or scientific reasons, instead of political motivations (Gibson et al. 1998, 345).

Furthermore, the age of the Court is not necessarily related to the salience of it. Salience is more present in Courts that make decisions with public impact, rather than on arcane legal issues. As a result, the number of cases of mass attention, the exposure of legitimising symbols and the opportunities to reach audiences, such as public hearings, are measures of the salience of a Court.

The way salience may be operationalised is by measuring whether individuals have heard of the JEP in general. Moreover, it is important to study if they know how this complex system works (e.g. how it combines restorative and retributive justice, uses a system of benefits to encourage the *comparecientes*' contribution to the victims' rights, and sanctions only those most responsible for the studied crimes).

4.2.3 *Obedience*

The obedience of decisions is an essential matter to the legitimacy of a judicial institution. Weber called this rulership—"the chance that specific (or all) commands will be met with obedience on the part of a specifiable group of persons" (2019, 134). If individuals and institutions decide not to enforce and comply with the rulings, the legitimacy of a Court is at stake because, as Gibson et al. have pointed out, it does not have the power of the purse—it does not decide on its own budget—or the sword—the compliance of its decisions hinges on the government (1998, 343). In consequence, for the enforcement of their rulings and support, Courts rely on the goodwill of the Executive and Legislative branches and of society in general.

To operationalise this element, I identify remarkable cases where the rulings of the JEP have not been fulfilled. I checked "remarkable cases" because they are the only ones identifiable through the media. Others are nearly impossible to trace with the available means to do this research.

4.2.4 *Age*

The age of a Tribunal can be relevant to the legitimacy of a judicial institution. Gibson et al. posited that diffuse support is achieved through the consistent results of a Court, namely "the slow accretion of positive messages about courts and law" (Gibson et al. 1998, 345). Thus, according to them, older high courts tend to have more legitimacy than younger courts.

This is an important factor to consider because the JEP is one of its kind: it is a new jurisdiction, created from scratch and delivering transitional justice, with more favourable opinions than older judicial institutions, and at the same time it is conceived to finish its operations after a certain period. For example, according to the April 2024 Invamer poll (a poll on public opinion held consistently since 1994 and based on the Gallup Poll), the Supreme Court, the oldest of the Colombian High Courts, created in its current form in 1886, had the favourable opinion of 31% of the respondents, while 39% of the respondents had positive opinions on the JEP, which started its operation only in 2018.

The way to operationalise age is to document changes in people's support over time. This measurement reflects how age impacts the goodwill reservoir of a Court.

4.2.5 *Measurement of the Legitimacy Factors*

Now that all five factors are explained, I will organise their signs in a table for the sake of clarity. To build the table, I followed Pion-Berlin's example (1994). In 1994, he studied the variables that had made Argentina hold trials against human rights offenders, unlike Chile and Uruguay. He summarised his data in a table and gauged their importance to produce the outcome. Similarly, the following table summarises the factors that strengthen or erode legitimacy with their respective signs (Table 4.1).

These signs are useful to gauge whether the JEP's legitimacy is strengthening or eroding over time. As it was stated before, legitimacy capital is dynamic: it changes over time with every action of the system's actors—the JEP, victims, *comparecientes,* Government. Those actions might trigger the signs of strength or erosion of the JEP's legitimacy, promoting a change in the JEP's legitimacy. Those who were previous supporters might become critics. For instance, this has occurred since February 2024 with the last living members of the FARC Secretariat and some of the former Government's peace negotiators, as I show Sect. 5.2.7.

Moreover, these signs can change not only over time but also across social groups. As a result, different social groups may have different understandings of the JEP's legitimacy. However, this table and the

Table 4.1 Factors that strengthen or erode the JEP's legitimacy

Factors	*Signs of legitimacy strengthening*	*Signs of legitimacy erosion*
Diffuse support	• Evidence of rejection to make fundamental changes to the JEP • Signs that the international community supports the JEP's operation and that it does not accept any fundamental change • Acceptance of contentious decisions • Trust in the JEP	• Consensus to change the JEP among political actors, scholars and experts • Reaction to changes in the budget allocated to the JEP • Resistance to contentious decisions • Mistrust in the JEP
Specific support	• Framing of the JEP's decisions • Number of victims participating in the macro-cases • Satisfaction across social groups • Speed in handing down decisions • Equity in investigations between Armed Forces and FARC-EP	• Victims dropping out of the JEP • Strong consistent critiques of the JEP • Salient cases of opposition to the JEP because of its decisions
Obedience/ Rulership	• Obedience of its decisions • Reactions to the hearings of the JEP	• Reluctance to fulfil the decisions
Salience	• Understanding of the JEP, especially of restorative justice • Number of cases of mass attention • Exposure to legitimising symbols	• Number of people who do not understand the JEP and the purpose and means of restorative justice • Signs that individuals do not know of the JEP's existence
Age of the institution	• Age of the JEP • Signs of increasing and decreasing support over time	• Eroded authority because of the institution's age

following scale are of use because they provide a practical tool that effectively estimates the JEP's legitimacy and could weigh the legitimacy of any other judicial institution of transitional justice in other countries.

Yet, these indicators by themselves are not enough to gauge the legitimacy of the JEP. It is necessary to measure and weigh them. To begin with, the JEP's legitimacy should not be gauged as a binary value—that the JEP is legitimate or the JEP is not legitimate. Rather, as the result of several factors, it should be estimated in degrees, considering that the factors have different weights according to their importance. The following scale is a tool that fulfils that goal. It integrates the different legitimacy factors and measures the extent to which they are present (Table 4.2).

This scale draws on Payne et al.'s accountability scale for cases of human rights violations committed by corporations (2020). They built a progressive scale to measure the extent of accountability of the cases of alleged corporate responsibility they had collected on a database. They

Table 4.2 Scale of the JEP's sociological legitimacy

Degree			
Item	*1—Low*	*2—Medium*	*3—High*
Diffuse support	Individuals are willing to make fundamental changes to the JEP Individuals do not accept contentious decisions Individuals mistrust the JEP	Most individuals are willing to make fundamental changes to the JEP They accept contentious decisions Individuals somewhat trust the JEP	Most individuals are unwilling to make fundamental changes to the JEP They accept contentious decisions Individuals trust the JEP
Specific support	Most individuals are dissatisfied with the JEP's decisions Most individuals refuse restorative justice They have strong critiques to the decisions	Most individuals are somewhat satisfied with the JEP's decisions Most individuals somehow accept restorative justice Some have major critiques	Most individuals are satisfied with the decisions Most individuals accept restorative justice Some have minor critiques
Obedience	Authorities and individuals do not obey any decision	Authorities and individuals obey most decisions. Few cases of disobedience	Authorities and individuals obey all decisions
Salience	Most individuals have not heard of the JEP The majority does not know how the JEP works (restorative justice, selective justice, systems of benefits, etc.)	Most individuals have heard of the JEP They somewhat know how the JEP works (restorative justice, selective justice, systems of benefits, etc.)	Most individuals have heard of the JEP They know how it works (restorative justice, selective justice, systems of benefits, etc.)
Age	The age of the JEP at the moment of measurement		

ranged them in five categories: from no accountability (when State agencies and international governmental organisations had started to collect evidence) to very high accountability (when processes had final convictions or civil judgements). A similar procedure was followed by Shenk (2022). She proposed five stages of progress towards the implementation of *consultas populares*, a democratic mechanism whereby communities across Colombia used to vote to decide about extractivist projects in their territories. In the same vein, I propose a scale to measure the extent of the JEP's legitimacy by assessing the presence of the factors of diffuse support, specific support, obedience, salience and age.

References

Beetham, David. 2002. *The Legitimation of Power*. 5th print. Issues in Political Theory. Macmillan.

Botero, Sandra. 2020. "Trust in Colombia's Justicia Especial Para La Paz: Experimental Evidence." *Journal of Politics in Latin America* 12 (3): 300–322. https://doi.org/10.1177/1866802X20959509.

Cohen, Harlan Grant, Andreas Follesdal, Nienke Grossman, and Geir Ulfstein. 2018. "Legitimacy and International Courts – A Framework." In *Legitimacy and International Courts*, 1st ed., edited by Nienke Grossman, Harlan Grant Cohen, Andreas Follesdal, and Geir Ulfstein. Cambridge University Press. https://doi.org/10.1017/9781108529570.001.

De la Calle Lombana, Humberto. 2019. *Revelaciones al Final de Una Guerra: Testimonio Del Jefe Negociador Del Gobierno Colombiano En La Habana*. DEBATE.

Easton, David. 1975. "A Re-Assessment of the Concept of Political Support." *British Journal of Political Science* 5 (4): 435–57. https://doi.org/10.1017/S0007123400008309.

El Espectador. 2020. "Pasados cuatro años del plebiscito que dividió a Colombia." Text. ELESPECTADOR.COM, October 2. https://www.elespectador.com/politica/pasados-cuatro-anos-del-plebiscito-que-dividio-a-colombia-article/.

Forero-Alba, Sofía, and Juan Carlos Rodríguez-Raga. 2022. "Courting Judicial Legitimacy: An Experimental Study of the Colombian Constitutional Court." In *The Limits of Judicialization*, 1st ed., edited by Sandra Botero, Daniel M. Brinks, and Ezequiel A. Gonzalez-Ocantos. Cambridge University Press. https://doi.org/10.1017/9781009093859.007.

Galtung, Johan. 1969. "Violence, Peace, and Peace Research." *Journal of Peace Research* 6 (3): 167–91. https://doi.org/10.1177/002234336900600301.

Gibson, James L., and Gregory A. Caldeira. 2003. "Defenders of Democracy? Legitimacy, Popular Acceptance, and the South African Constitutional Court." *The Journal of Politics* 65 (1): 1–30. https://doi.org/10.1111/1468-2508.t01-1-00001.

Gibson, James, Gregory Caldeira, and Vanessa Baird. 1998. "On the Legitimacy of National High Courts." *The American Political Science Review* 92 (June): 343. https://doi.org/10.2307/2585668.

Gómez, Gabriel Ignacio. 2022. "Political Conflicts over the JEP: A Sociolegal Perspective." In *Transitional Justice in Colombia: The Special Jurisdiction for Peace [Electronic Resource]*, edited by Kai Ambos and Stefan Peters, with Susann Aboueldahab. Studien Zu Lateinamerika; Volume 44. Nomos. https://directory.doabooks.org/handle/20.500.12854/81931.

Gomez-Suarez, Andrei. 2016. *El triunfo del no: la paradoja emocional detrás del plebiscito*. Paradoja emocional detrás del plebiscito. Icono.

Lupu, Yonatan. 2013. "International Judicial Legitimacy: Lessons from National Courts." *Theoretical Inquiries in Law* 14 (2). https://doi.org/10.1515/til-2013-022.

Nelson, Thomas E., Rosalee A. Clawson, and Zoe M. Oxley. 1997. "Media Framing of a Civil Liberties Conflict and Its Effect on Tolerance." *American Political Science Review* 91 (3): 567–83. https://doi.org/10.2307/2952075.

Payne, Leigh A., Gabriel Pereira, and Laura Bernal-Bermúdez. 2020. *Transitional Justice and Corporate Accountability from Below: Deploying Archimedes' Lever*. Cambridge University Press. Cambridge Core. https://doi.org/10.1017/9781108564564.

Pianigiani, Ottorino. 1907. Vocabolario etimologico della lingua italiana. In *Vocabolario etimologico della lingua italiana*. Società editrice Dante Alighieri di Albrighi, Segati. https://www.etimo.it/?term=legittimo.

Pion-Berlin, David. 1994. "To Prosecute or to Pardon? Human Rights Decisions in the Latin American Southern Cone." *Human Rights Quarterly* 16 (1): 105. https://doi.org/10.2307/762413.

Santos, Juan Manuel. 2019. *La Batalla Por La Paz*. Grupo Planeta - Colombia.

Shany, Yuval. 2014. *Assessing the Effectiveness of International Courts*. Oxford University Press. https://doi.org/10.1093/acprof:oso/9780199643295.001.0001.

Shenk, J. L. 2022. "Democratization from below: Citizen-Activated Participatory Democracy in Colombia's Extractive Industries." PhD Thesis, University of Oxford.

Valencia Valencia, Paula Andrea, and Pedro Francés-Gómez. 2018. "Legitimidad de la Jurisdicción Especial para la Paz." *Revista de Paz y Conflictos* 11 (1): 105–33. https://doi.org/10.30827/revpaz.v11i1.6027.

Voeten, Erik. 2013. "Public Opinion and the Legitimacy of International Courts." *Theoretical Inquiries in Law* (Tel Aviv) 14 (2): 411–36. https://doi.org/10.1515/til-2013-021.

Weber, Max. 2019. *Economy and Society: A New Translation*. With Keith Tribe. Ebook Central. Harvard University Press. https://ezproxy-prd.bodleian.ox.ac.uk/login?url=https://ebookcentral.proquest.com/lib/oxford/detail.action?docID=5715885.

Zartman, I William. 2001. "The Timing of Peace Initiatives: Hurting Stalemates and Ripe Moments[1]." *Global Review of Ethnopolitics* 1 (1): 8–18. https://doi.org/10.1080/14718800108405087.

CHAPTER 5

Legitimacy Factors

Abstract This chapter studies the signs of erosion and strengthening and gauges them on the scale. Considering these factors, the JEP has a medium level of legitimacy. Such a legitimacy could increase or decrease depending on the pressing issues, such as the lack of salience and definitive rulings, the efficacy of the *sanciones propias* or the satisfaction of the victims regarding their participation. Diffuse support is high because most individuals have not been willing to accept fundamental changes to the JEP, and contentious decisions are accepted. Moreover, a significant share of Colombians trust the JEP or have a favourable image of it. Lastly, many national and international organisations have confirmed and supported the JEP's operation. The JEP's specific support is medium verging on low. This factor is affected by the victims' satisfaction with proceedings; the delays in handing down decisions; the equal treatment in investigating both parties of the Peace Agreement; acceptance of restorative justice; and notable cases of dissatisfaction with the JEP's decisions. Salience is low, since most Colombians do not understand the JEP's operation, although many Colombians know about the existence of the JEP. Obedience ranges from medium to high, as most decisions are complied with, even the most controversial.

N. Zuluaga Afanador, *The Sociological Legitimacy of the Special Jurisdiction for Peace of Colombia*, St Antony's Series,
https://doi.org/10.1007/978-3-032-21912-1_5

Keywords Acceptance of restorative justice · Trust · International cooperation · Institutional salience · Tolerance to contentious decisions · Favourable opinion · Victims' participation · Armed Forces · FARC-EP

In this chapter, I develop the conceptual framework described earlier. Using the definition of every one of the factors, I probe into the signs of strengthening or eroding legitimacy. In the last section, I gauge the different factors using the proposed scale to assess the JEP's legitimacy.

5.1 Diffuse Support

5.1.1 Sociopolitical Willingness to Adopt Fundamental Changes to the JEP

Since its creation in 2017, and as of July 2026, the structure of the JEP has been significantly modified only by the Constitutional Court, which is in charge of guaranteeing the primacy of the Constitution and the protection of fundamental rights. In 2018, as it was studying the constitutionality of the JEP's by-laws, the Court ruled, among other modifications, that civilians and agents of the State could not be forced to appear before the JEP because this violated their right to a natural judge, namely to be investigated by the ordinary jurisdiction by default (Gutiérrez 2022, 76).

However, other actors have not been able to modify the JEP. Neither the Government nor Congress have been able to do so. There has not been a massive group of citizens promoting changes or opposing its operation. Rather, when the JEP's structure has been potentially adjusted, intellectuals and hundreds of citizens have mobilised to support the JEP's operation, as I will explain later. In other words, since the creation of the JEP, a sociopolitical unwillingness to modify the JEP has seemed to prevail.

This unwillingness can be observed in the institutional, political and civil reaction to former President Iván Duque's objections to the JEP's by-laws. Between the formal beginning of the operations of the JEP and the enactment of its by-laws, one year and three months passed. During that time, the justices and their staff had to make legal interpretations to make judicial decisions. Congress approved the by-laws of the JEP on November 28, 2017, and the Constitutional Court finished the study of constitutionality on December 19, 2018 (Constitutional Court of Colombia 2018). On March 11, 2019, President Duque presented six objections to such a Law. He asked for a more detailed regulation when it comes to the reparations, the competence of certifying the members of the FARC-EP and the faculty of the JEP to prevent the extradition of someone under its jurisdiction. Furthermore, he argued that crimes against humanity should be prosecuted in any case (Ámbito Jurídico 2019).

Given that most of those concerns had already been clarified by the Constitutional Court, many sectors of the society perceived Duque's objections as unfair and as a veiled obstacle to implementing the Peace Agreement. Thus, following Duque's interventions, there were several mobilisations across Colombia and even in Paris supporting the JEP.

Simultaneously, notorious figures manifested their support to the JEP. Antanas Mockus (a popular politician who was Major of Bogotá twice), Jesús Abad Colorado (a notorious armed conflict photojournalist), Juan Gabriel Vásquez (a famous Colombian writer) Carlos Negret (then Colombian ombudsman), Angélica Lozano (congresswoman at the time) and Cecilia López (former Minister of Agriculture), and many other intellectuals and public figures organised a campaign to support the JEP, under the hashtag #YoDefiendoLaJEP—#IDefendTheJEP—(BBC News Mundo 2019; Semana 2019a, b).

In the end, the House of Representatives rejected the objections, as well as the Senate. On May 30, 2019, the Constitutional Court ruled that the Senate had effectively rejected Duque's objections (BBC News Mundo 2019). As a result, it forced him to sign the Law on June 6, 2019. His attempt to modify the JEP's structure had failed.

In the following years, Centro Democrático, Duque's party, tried to modify the JEP several times. Senator Paloma Valencia, one of the leading voices at the CD, proposed to create a special panel to try members of the Armed Forces. His attempt, as well as other CD's legislative initiatives to simply eliminate the JEP, has failed (Semana 2020a).

5.1.2 Support from Other Institutions to Reinforce the JEP's Operation or to Protect It

Over time, the Prosecutor's Office of the International Criminal Court, the European Union and the Security Council of the United Nations (UN) have consistently funded, supported and approved the JEP. This support gives the JEP some institutional legitimacy that may translate into diffuse support.

For instance, Karim Khan, the current Prosecutor of the International Criminal Court (ICC), closed the preliminary examination of the situation in Colombian because he observed that the Government, the domestic judicial institution and especially the JEP have been progressing in the investigation and prosecution of Rome Statute crimes. As a result, he signed a cooperation agreement with the Colombian government for further complementarity between the two entities, maintaining the faculty to reconsider the situation of complementarity.

This agreement was the first of its kind in the history of the ICC and comprised commitments for both parties (International Criminal Court 2021). The Prosecutor's Office of the ICC announced its institutional support for Colombia's efforts on accountability. The Colombian Government committed to: (1) protecting, funding and supporting the structures that carry out accountability, including the JEP; (2) ensuring their independence; (3) safeguarding the security of prosecutorial and judicial personnel, and of those appearing before the different mechanisms; and (4) promoting cooperation among the different entities. In other words, this agreement internationally obliges the Colombian Government to fund, support and maintain the JEP's operation. It may also be a sign of diffuse support from the ICC. In consequence, the ICC has communicated the opening of an office in the JEP's offices (JEP Press Office 2023b) and on April 27 2024, Colombia and the ICC confirmed a policy agreement to enhance the Colombian system of transitional justice and encourage Colombia to share its example with the world (JEP Press Office 2024). In Khan's words, "the criminal model of Colombia is an example for the international criminal system" (La Silla Vacía 2024).

Not only the ICC, but also the UN Security Council has strongly supported the JEP's operation. In 2016, it established the UN Verification Mission to oversee the implementation of the Final Peace Agreement and, pertaining to the JEP, it has contributed to the compliance of *comparecientes'* restorative actions. Particularly, it has verified the compliance of the proper sanctions and has fostered the coordination among institutions in a Mechanism of Verification of proper sanctions (UN Verification Mission and JEP 2022).

Furthermore, while considering Colombia's sovereignty, the UN Security Council showed "vocal, consistent but measured support for the JEP during a crucial period when it was under attack", namely when former President Duque objected to the by-laws of the JEP (Rebecca Brubaker 2020, 53). At that time, it underlined the importance of protecting the JEP's legitimacy and independence without undermining the Government's right to object and allowed the Member States to express their concerns in that regard. For instance, the Netherlands, then a non-permanent member of the Council, stressed that it was of utmost importance to reduce legal uncertainty for former FARC-EP combatants to reduce their fear and provide access to transitional justice (Rebecca Brubaker 2020, 60). In the interviews I conducted, several JEP justices confirmed that international support was essential to establishing the JEP, especially in its first years.[1]

The EU and some of its members, like Sweden and Germany, have also actively funded the JEP's operation. In 2020, the EU allocated 3.5 million euros to invest in strategic actions of the JEP (Semana 2020b). In the following years, it also hired many analysts to speed up the investigations of the macro-cases and provided economic support to some FARC-EP ex-members as their amnesties are pending (Ospina-Pedraza et al. 2023).

To sum up, the international community's support has been essential to the JEP's legitimacy, especially when former President Duque objected to the Statutory Law, questioning both the legal and sociological legitimacy of the JEP. At that time, the UN Security Council's strategic support to the JEP's independence and autonomy acted as a boundary to the intentions of the Government. Later, in 2022, the ICC agreement formally and internationally obliged the Colombian Government to respect the JEP's independence and autonomy, and to properly fund it to avoid resuming the preliminary examinations. After such an agreement, no significant changes to the JEP have been consistently proposed. The EU's operational support has also helped the JEP to speed up its investigations.

[1] Pedro Elías Díaz, interview by author, Bogotá, 08/02/2023. Óscar Parra Vera, interview by author, Oxford, 10/03/2024. Alejandro Ramelli, interview by author, Bogotá, 07/26/2023.

5.1.3 *Tolerance to Contentious Decisions*

The Santrich Case

The Santrich case is a good example of how, in May 2019, Colombian society and institutions reacted to arguably the most contentious decision the JEP has made. Seuxis Pausias Hernández Solarte "Jesús Santrich" had been detained since April 2018 as a result of a DEA's extradition request for his potential participation in drug trafficking. On May 16, 2019, the JEP released him for not having enough evidence to establish the time when the alleged crimes had been committed.

"Jesús Santrich" was particularly controversial because he showed signs of disregard towards the victims and did not cooperate with the JEP. On the day the peace negotiations were announced, in October 2012, he was asked whether the FARC-EP would provide remedies to the victims and jocularly replied "quizás, quizás, quizás"—"perhaps, perhaps, perhaps"—alluding to a very popular song.[2] This caused major distress and discontent among the victims (Semana 2021).

Moreover, he never cooperated with the JEP. In the macro-case on kidnappings, in the second half of 2018, Julieta Lemaitre, the leading justice of the case, summoned him to give his version of the crimes committed. But he never appeared before the court (El País 2018).

He was supposed to take office as a congressman in July 2018 but was never able to do so. Almost one month after the JEP started operating, on April 10, 2018, "Jesús Santrich" was captured in Bogotá, following an Interpol request and put in preventive detention. The United States Justice Department argued that he was responsible for planning the trafficking of 10 tons of cocaine to the United States with Marlon Márquez, nephew of Iván Márquez, the former FARC-EP chief peace negotiator.

The President of the time, Juan Manuel Santos, stated that if the crime was proved, he would not hesitate in extraditing "Santrich". As a former FARC-EP member, "Santrich" had the right not to be extradited for crimes committed before November 26, 2016. Therefore, the JEP had to decide whether the alleged accusations happened before or after that date. In the second case, his case would be adjudicated by the ordinary justice and he could have got extradited (Semana 2018).

[2] "Quizás, quizás, quizás" is a song written by Osvaldo Farrés in 1947 and famously interpreted by Trío Los Panchos. It is very popular in Colombian culture.

The JEP requested evidence in order to rule. Even though videos of "Santrich" planning the operation were leaked to the press, neither the United State Justice Department nor the Attorney General's Office of Colombia presented any evidence of the crime before the JEP. Consequently, on May 16, 2019, the JEP ruled that "Santrich" should not be extradited because there were no grounds to establish the date of the alleged crimes. Since there were doubts on the date of the alleged crimes, he could not be extradited (JEP Press Office 2019a). Arguing that the JEP's decision breached the Colombian Law system, Néstor Humberto Martínez, Attorney General at the time, resigned (El País 2019).

This situation prompted institutional tension and eroded the JEP's image, but also proved that it could act as a veto player, ensuring its independence and autonomy (Gibson and Caldeira 2003). In spite of Martínez' allegations, the JEP's ruling was mostly complied with.

As "Santrich" was going out of jail, he was arrested again. This time the Attorney General's Office sought to prosecute him not according to an extradition request, but to Colombian Law. A few days later, and deciding with the available evidence, the Supreme Court ruled that "Santrich" should be released from jail because there was no risk of escape. Thus, he took office as congressman on June 11, 2019.

In the following months, he disappeared and staged a video along with Luciano Marin Arango "Iván Márquez", former chief negotiator of the FARC-EP Peace delegation, and *compareciente* before the JEP. They proclaimed the creation of the "Second Marquetalia", an armed resurrection of the FARC-EP, because, in their opinion, the Government breached its compromises as part of the Peace Agreement. In consequence, they were expelled from the JEP for taking up arms again, and their cases were returned to ordinary Courts. "Santrich" was killed by the Colombian Army on May 18 2021 (BBC News Mundo 2021). Nowadays, the Segunda Marquetalia is one of the organised armed groups that has been negotiating with the Petro Government for a peace deal.

In March 2023, the JEP filed a criminal complaint against some officers of the Attorney General's Office, after a forensic study of Guernica Chambers, an English law firm, established there were many irregularities in the case. Precisely, one of the motivations of the JEP to act was to clarify that episode, which may have affected the JEP's image, as it is observable in the Invamer Polls presented in the Image 5.2 (JEP Press Office 2023a).

The fact that the JEP's legitimacy can withstand contentious decisions does not mean that it does not get eroded by them. Observing the Invamer Poll, a survey conducted every two months following Gallup poll's standards about public opinions on political leaders and institutions, it is possible to see that after the JEP took the Santrich case's final decision, favourable opinion dropped from 46% of the respondents to 36%.

Does that mean that this decision was the cause of the erosion of legitimacy? Not necessarily. In May 2019 Congress was discussing Duque's objections, which might also be a cause of such a drop. This example shows the difficulty in assessing diffuse support and the reaction to contentious decisions without further data. Thus, I opted also to identify substantial facts that could account for tolerance or intolerance to contentious rulings, such as mobilisations, disobedience to the decisions and major reactions of the actors within the JEP's system. Since, as far as I could establish, none of them occurred, it is possible to say that, in general, Colombian society and institutions tolerated the suspension of Santrich's extradition.

The Santrich case provides a concrete example of the JEP's ability to remain legitimate despite unpopular decisions. First, the JEP's decision to guarantee the non-extradition of Santrich was handed down while Congress was debating Duque's objections. Regardless of such a controversial decision, Congress refused to change the JEP's by-laws.

Second, despite being a very contentious matter, the media coverage was somewhat favourable to the JEP, showing the Government's and the Attorney General's negligence in getting the evidence from the US Justice Department. In fact, after sifting through the articles about the JEP in Semana,[3] I found that its coverage is somewhat favourable. At the beginning of the process, in April 2018, the magazine was critical about the decision of the JEP to suspend the extradition. Over time, it included interviews with several experts and reported on the case's progress, allowing the JEP and the Attorney General to present their point of view. When the JEP made its ruling, the magazine did not directly criticise the decision (Image 5.1).

[3] It is important to note that Semana has been the most critical media of the JEP after Gabriel Gilinski, one of the richest men in Colombia, bought most of its shares in January 2019.

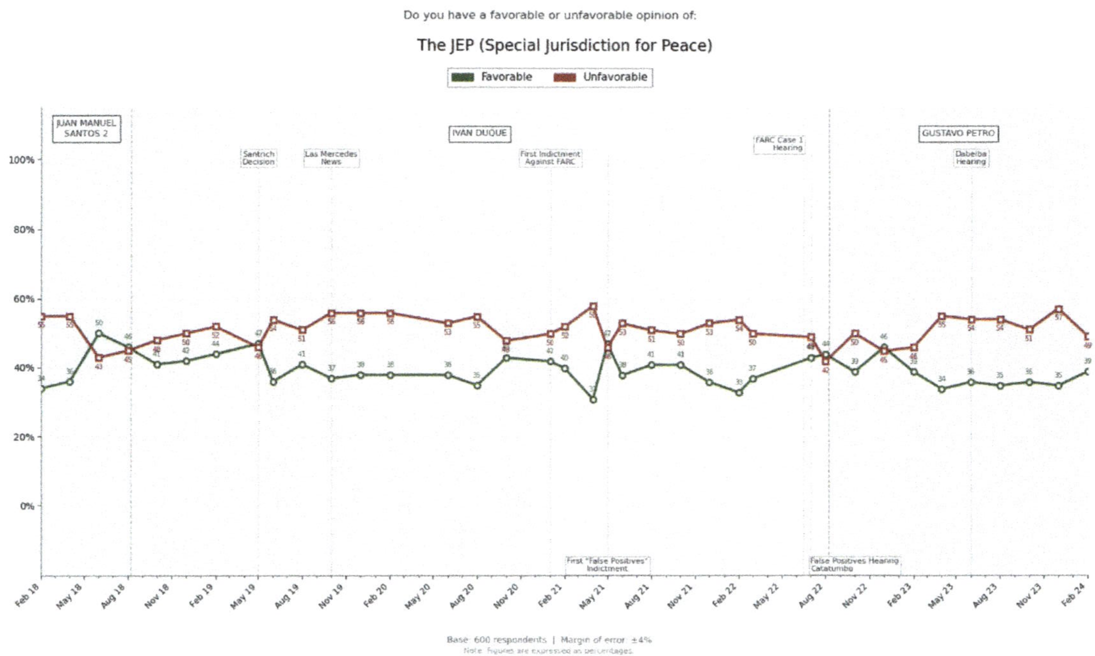

Image 5.1 Favourable or unfavourable opinion regarding the JEP (*Source* Graph by the author, based on Invamer [2024])

5.1.4 *Trust and Favourable Opinion Towards the JEP*

The literature has consistently argued that trust in courts and support towards them may strengthen their ability to act independently and the acceptance of their rulings (Botero 2020; Easton 1975; Gibson and Caldeira 2003). Moreover, popular support may be even more important for transitional courts. These tribunals are frequently new institutions that operate in politicised environments. Their decisions are heavily scrutinised by victims, political stakeholders and civil society organisations. Conversely, distrust can erode their credibility, encourage political discontent and hinder the peace process' implementation (Botero 2020, 302).

The only survey that explicitly asked respondents about their trust towards the JEP has been the Democracy Report by the Americas Barometer in 2018 and 2023. The results are as follows (Image 5.2).

Responses ranged from one to seven, where one indicated "nothing" and seven "very much". If we consider that only those who responded five, six or seven trust in the JEP, only 37% of participants expressed trust

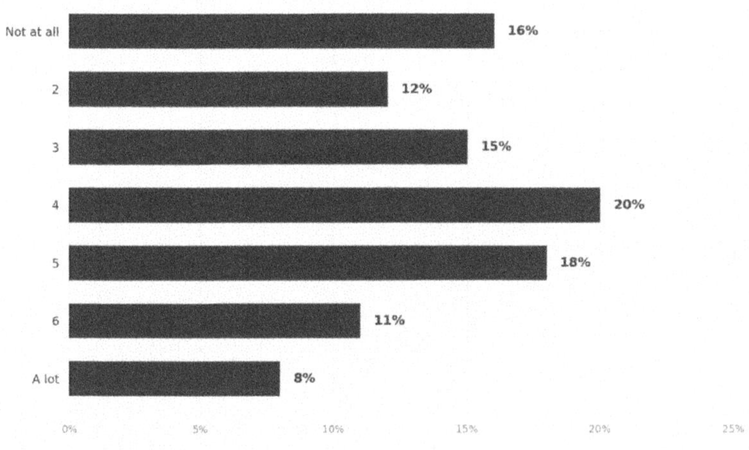

Image 5.2 To what extent do you trust the JEP? (*Source* Graph by the author, based on Rodríguez-Raga [2023])

in the institution (Rodríguez-Raga 2023, 49). This represents a reduction by 5 percentage points from 2018. In 2023, the most common response was neutral—neither trust nor mistrust the JEP—chosen by 20% of respondents, while 43% expressed mistrust in the JEP. Although the minority trusts the JEP, there is room for growth, particularly among the 20% who neither trust nor mistrust the JEP, rating four in the survey.

Consistent with the literature, familiarity with the JEP's operations impacts trust. Among those who reported understanding the JEP's functioning, the proportion of those who trust the JEP is two times larger than those who do not. Moreover, those who are more likely to trust the JEP have a several characteristics. They self-identify as left-wing, live in rural areas and have lower levels of formal education (2023, 49).

It is difficult to assess whether these are high numbers compared to other transitional justice cases, as, to my knowledge, there are no other surveys on trust in transitional justice courts. That is why I will compare these data with the favourable opinion on other Colombian judicial institutions using the Invamer Poll, which has been measuring this item since 2000 (Invamer 2024).

To begin with, the Americas Barometer's data aligns with Invamer Poll's reports on favourable opinion of judicial institutions. In February 2024, 39% of the respondents had a favourable opinion of the JEP versus 49% who reported an unfavourable view, showing similar indicators (Invamer 2024).

During its existence, the JEP has been the second judicial institution with the most favourable image after the Constitutional Court—arguably the most powerful and prestigious judicial institution in Colombia. Between one month before the beginning of the JEP's operation, February 2018, and the February 2024 poll, the favourable opinion regarding the JEP fluctuated between 31% of the total respondents (April 2021) and 50% (June 2018).

In contrast, favourable opinions of the Attorney General's Office ranged from 22% (August 2021) to 47% (October 2018), and scored 34% in the last study. The Supreme Court's image followed a similar trend with favourability ranging from 18%, in February 2022, to 40%, in August 2020, and scoring 31% in the last poll—ten points lower than the JEP. As for the Constitutional Court, the favourable opinion peaked in February 2019 at 47%, plummeted to a low of 25% in February 2022 and rose to 44% in the last poll (February 2024).

Overall, at least 1 out of 3 Colombians either trust the JEP or have a favourable image of it. Trust is more present in rural areas, among people with lower educational level, and self-identified as left-wing (Rodríguez-Raga 2023, 49). Although these number may seem small, compared to other judicial institutions, the JEP has the second most favourable opinion. As the literature has suggested, increasing the salience and knowledge of the JEP can foster trust. The 20% of the respondents who neither trust nor mistrust the JEP are a potential audience for trust-building measures.

5.2 Specific Support

To understand the extent of social support for the JEP's rulings, it is essential to analyse the major factors that influence its support or rejection. As there was no guidance in the transitional justice and JEP academic literature, I propose some elements that affect specific support in the JEP's case.

Analysing the conducted interviews, news, and social media, I looked for similarities in the responses across constituencies with different ideological views. Receiving similar responses despite opposing views increased the chances of identifying a reliable factor. The proposed factors may contribute to assess other transitional justice institutions' legitimacy.

As a result of this analysis process, in this section, I will probe into: (1) the victims' satisfaction with some cases of the JEP; (2) the victims' participation; (3) the delays in handing down decisions; (4) the equal treatment in investigating, adjudicating and sanctioning both parties of the Peace Agreement; (5) the importance of reaching acceptance of restorative justice; and (6) cases of dissatisfaction with the JEP's decisions.

5.2.1 Victims' Satisfaction in Certain JEP Cases

To assess the satisfaction of victims in the JEP's cases is nearly an impossible task. Thousands of victims are recognised in the JEP's proceedings—as is shown in the tables of the Sect. 3.4—and they are heterogeneous—they were victimised by different actors, come from different regions and belong to different ethnic groups. However, I argue that it is possible to have an idea of the victims' satisfaction with some of the JEP's proceedings by analysing the interviews of victims of different actors, victims' attorneys, intellectuals and some of the JEP justices.

After analysing victims' interviews and observing hearings, I suggest that victims are more likely to be satisfied with the JEP's operation if the case provides new information or effectively benefits them.

Esneda Altamirán's case is one example of this.[4] She is one of the victims in the milestone case of Dabeiba, within the macro-case 3 for *falsos positivos*. Interviews to Armed Forces agents within the macro-cases 3 for *falsos positivos* helped the JEP discover many bodies of disappeared people in 2019, at Las Mercedes cemetery at Dabeiba, a municipality in the Urabá region. The body of John Arvy Cañas Cano, Esneda's nephew, was one of them.

This process not only helped Esneda's family recover Jhon Arvy's remains, but also changed Esneda's beliefs. She explained that, before participating in the JEP, she had opposed to the Peace Agreement, even voting against it in the referendum. By her account, she only echoed what she heard in the streets and from her husband, she remained suspicious when she began participating in the JEP's preparatory meetings. Gradually, as she received psychosocial support, having spaces where her concerns were heard and she was prepared for the different stages of the process, she trusted the JEP more and more. Over time, she became one of the speakers at Dabeiba's Hearing for the Acknowledgement of Responsibility and Truth (ARVR), at which eight former Army members accepted responsibility for killing and disappearing 47 people between 2002 and 2006.

A case of a FARC-EP victim is very different.[5] The FARC-EP kidnapped her father when she was 16 and later they killed him under circumstances that she does not feel have been clarified enough. She thinks that the *comparecientes* have not provided sufficient truth. Similarly, many other victims of that macro-case mistrust the former FARC-EP members, and in some cases they have dropped out of the JEP. In general, she accepts that the JEP helps to clarify the truth. But it is a slow process, and she feels that she could have more participation in processes before ordinary courts.

The stark difference could be explained by the fact that Esneda's case had not been prosecuted before and, thanks to the JEP, she could partially bring closure to the victimisation experience following her nephew's body

[4] Esneda Altamiranda, interview by author, Online, 08/10/2023.

[5] Interviewee 34, interview by author, Bogotá, 08/14/2023.

identification. In contrast, the victim of the second case has not been able to reach closure. She does not feel satisfied with the truth *comparecientes* have provided: the circumstances of her father's killing are still unclear. Moreover, her case was previously processed by the ordinary courts. In other words, as JEP justices Gustavo Salazar[6] and Alejandro Ramelli[7] suggested, the JEP strengthens its legitimacy when it can provide something new to society. The victims are more satisfied when the truth they receive helps them reach an emotional closure.

The cultural adoption of a provisional number of *falsos positivos* is another proof that society is more satisfied with the JEP's rulings when it acquires new information. On February 12 2021, the JEP provisionally established that 6,402 civilians had been illegally killed by the Armed Forces between 2002 and 2008. This number was significantly higher than those previously reported by other institutions. Thus, several victims' organisations, especially one of the first *falsos positivos* victims' organisations MAFAPO (*Madres de Falsos Positivos de Soacha y Bogotá* / "Mothers of *Falsos Positivos* of Soacha and Bogotá"), have adopted such data to start a "Campaign for the Truth", putting up posters with the number 6,402 on some busy streets in Colombia's main cities. As shown in Image 5.4, the posters also asked the question "*¿Quién dio la orden?* / Who gave the order [of the killings]".

Another notable case is the one that occurred during the Paro Nacional of 2021, a series of protests against the National Government that lasted several months. During that time, the outreach of the *falsos positivos* estimation number went beyond the victims. For instance, protesters wrote "6,402 heroes" in the salient Monument of the Heroes in Bogotá as an act of rebellion. This was replicated in other places in Bogotá and Medellín (Mauricio Albarracín Caballero [@malbarracin] 2021; Justice for Colombia [@JFColombia] 2021). In other words, the number 6,402 became a symbol of discontent by displaying how corruption in Government had led to the death of thousands of young people in the past.

It may seem that progress on *falsos positivos* cases produces more legitimacy than progress on cases involving the FARC-EP. Why has the number of people kidnapped by the FARC between 1993 and 2012 (21,396) not

[6] Gustavo Salazar, interview by author, Bogotá, 08/08/2023. Justice Salazar is the coordinator of the macro-case 6.

[7] Ramelli, interview. Justice Ramelli is the coordinator of the Dabeiba case.

been as culturally embraced as 6,402 *falsos positivos*? Why, in the cases of the two interviewees I discussed here, is the person victimised by the FARC-EP less satisfied?

The figure of 6,402 may have resonated so strongly with Colombian society because it revealed that the scale of *falsos positivos* was far greater than what was hitherto perceived. The crimes were committed by the forces that should protect citizens, and for most citizens this was unexpected. This revelation challenged the narrative that *falsos positivos* were not a generalised practice. The narrative was reinforced by president Uribe's statement regarding the first widely publicised case of *falsos positivos* in 2007. He said that a dozen young people "were not going to pick coffee; they were going for criminal purposes",[8] referring to several poor youths from Soacha, a marginalised city near Bogotá, who were later found dead in Ocaña—hundreds of kilometres from their homes (AP News 2021) (Image 5.3).

In contrast, it was already known that the FARC-EP had massively kidnapped civilians. In fact, in the late 90s, roads were less used due to the fear that families would be kidnapped. Besides, it was somehow expected, not justified, that a guerrilla carried out those crimes.

It may also be the case that some victims of the Armed Forces are more satisfied with the JEP's rulings because the truth they receive allows them to find closure from their trauma. When the interviews were conducted (June through September 2023), the truth being provided by the FARC-EP may have been less satisfying. Many of former guerrilla members, and even commanders, were killed during the war; others betrayed the Peace Agreement, with them much truth was lost. Moreover, the strategy of macro-case one proceeds from the top to the bottom of the guerrilla hierarchy. By August 2023, in the ARVR, victims had heard only the versions of top commanders who usually do not know the details of their relatives' individual cases. It was not until April 2024 the first regional ARVR was held, in Ibagué.

In contrast, the *falsos positivos'* case is investigated from the bottom to the top of the military structure and many of the involved combatants were still alive at the time of the proceedings. Thus, at the time of the interviews, both Armed Forces agents and civilians were able to provide more detailed accounts of the events at the ARVRs. Perhaps these fuller

[8] Original quote: "No fueron a recoger café, iban con propósitos delincuenciales". Translation by the author.

Image 5.3 Piece from the Campaign "¿Quién dio la orden? / 'Who gave the order?'". 2021 (*Source* Author's own photograph)

description of the events contributed to a deeper sense of restoration for the victims.

5.2.2 *Victims' Participation in the JEP's Proceedings*

As I have stated before and is established in Article 13 of the Statutory Law, the victims' rights and especially providing them with restorative measures are some of the essential axes of the JEP's proceedings. As a result, the JEP has: (1) published a Handbook for integral victim's participation; (2) opened many territorial offices; (3) offered psychosocial assistance to the victims; and (4) fostered victims' participation as much as possible in hearings, interviews, the opening of cases, and other procedural opportunities.

Many of the interviewees across different sectors also agree that victim participation of the victims in these processes is essential. With adequate mechanisms, victims can provide feedback to the judges about whether the system's operation is meeting their needs and expectations. This information may help judges tailor their decisions and proceedings to better respond to these needs. When such measures are taken, the immediate users of the system may recognise greater social authority in the institution to rule on their conflicts, as its operation resonates with their needs. As Theodor Meron, former President of the International Criminal Tribunal for the former Yugoslavia, noted: "Trials which are conducted in the area itself, close to the victims, close to the crimes, have a greater resonance for the victims than trials which are conducted 2,000 miles away" (Meron 2003). Similarly, the closer the JEP's transitional judges come to addressing the victims' needs, the more impactful and legitimate their rulings may be. This perspective may explain the JEP's efforts to hold hearings in the affected territories—Dabeiba, Ocaña, and Yopal, among others—and to employ symbols and other framing strategies to connect more deeply with victims and broader audiences, as will be analysed in Sect. 5.2.4.

For example, after initially denying such a space, the JEP ultimately granted victims the opportunity to ask questions directly to former combatants during SRVR interviews (JEP Press Office 2019b). As a result, the SRVR began to offer space to *demandas de verdad* ("truth requests") allowing victims to directly request information from those presumed perpetrators. These spaces have been useful in many ways: some of them have helped the Panel find voids in the perpetrators' version, while others have helped the victims bring closure to their traumas.

Despite the JEP's efforts to foster the victims' participation, in August 2023, Paola Molano, then coordinator of the area of Transitional Justice at the well-known think-thank Dejusticia, argued that, for the victims, their participation is not enough.[9] Some felt that they had more participation before ordinary courts, as in the FARC-EP victim's case I mentioned above. Molano has observed that victims might become more frustrated as the process advances, underlying that curbing expectations is

[9] Paola Molano, interview by author, Online, 08/01/2023.

essential. Furthermore, in April and May 2023, Daniel Vargas[10] and Sebastián Escobar,[11] respective attorneys of the human rights organisations "Comisión Colombiana de Juristas" and "Colectivo de Abogados José Alvear Restrepo" at the moment of the interviews, agreed that the JEP had curtailed the victims' participation through the Ruling of Interpretation 3 of 2022 (*Sentencia interpretativa 3 de 2022*) by preventing the victims from using legal means to attack the rulings. For instance, following this decision, victims are not allowed to order an appeal to the indictments of those most responsible. The JEP based the decision on the principle of "strict temporality"—the acknowledgement that the JEP must adapt its operation to honour its limited existence in time.

Described also by one justice of the SRVR,[12] this situation consolidates a trade-off between the victims' participation and the JEP's speed in handing down decisions. The more the victims participate, the longer the JEP takes to rule on a case, which is important because it has a "strict temporality". Therefore, justices must find a balance between those two principles.

5.2.3 *Delays in Handing Down Final Rulings*

The delays of the JEP in reaching definitive rulings were pointed out by most of the interviewees as one of the main factors that affect legitimacy. I posit the delays and not the speed in handing down decisions as a factor, because quick decisions would not necessarily strengthen the JEP's legitimacy. The JEP might rule quickly on a case but rule in a controversial way. Rather, what erodes legitimacy are delays—not deciding in a reasonable time.

The victims might perceive delays as a synonym of impunity. Some of them have been partly satisfied by the actions of the JEP—be they the interviews to the potential perpetrators, the restorative processes of acknowledgement of truth and responsibility, or another of the JEP's actions. Yet, many others have assumed the costs of participating in the procedures and have not seen any sentence or closure of a case in the seven years of the JEP's operation. As Santiago Rodríguez, the journalist

[10] Daniel Vargas, interview by author, Online, 07/05/2023.

[11] Sebastián Escobar, interview by author, Online, 09/04/2023.

[12] Interviewee 11, interview by author, Bogotá, 08/30/2023.

who had covered the JEP between 2021 and 2024 at La Silla Vacía, said in 2023, "five years and the JEP has not concluded anything".[13] Wilson Ortiz,[14] attorney of Armed Forces *comparecientes* and victims, also pointed out: in the JEP, "there is not much solved. There is no implementation."[15] In fact, the data are quite indicative even two years later: as recognised by the JEP itself, during its more than seven years of operation, as of May 2, 2025, the JEP has not handed down any definitive rulings for those "most responsible", regardless of whether they were member of the FARC-EP or the Armed Forces, Agents of the State or civilians. When it comes to non-most-responsible *comparecientes*, the situation is somehow different but not particularly encouraging. As reported before, as of May 2, 2025, the SDSJ had granted definitive legal benefits to only 161 individuals out of the 6,319 it had under its jurisdiction—involving 2.54% of the total.

Delays in handing down definitive decisions only extend relevant discussions, such as if the imposition of a *sanción propia* is consistent with exercising political rights like being a congressman. Thus, for senator Paloma Valencia,[16] former President Iván Duque,[17] and Sofía Gaviria,[18] former congresswoman, a victim of the FARC-EP and former director of the Unit for the Attention of the Victims, the fact that some members of the FARC-EP are in office as congressmen proves that the JEP fosters impunity. In their view, not only they are at liberty when they should be in jail as most responsible for grave human rights violations, but they are rewarded with seats in Congress. Delays in handing down sentences against those deemed as most responsible are rendering discussions about the compatibility of proper sanctions with political participation moot. *Comunes*, the party created after the FARC-EP demobilisation, has ten granted seats in Congress until June 2026. By May 2025, former FARC-EP members identified as most responsible had been able to participate in

[13] Santiago Rodríguez, interview by author, Bogotá, 08/25/2023.

[14] Wilson Ortiz, interview by author, Online, 08/28/2023.

[15] Original quote: "No hay mucho resuelto. No hay implementación". Translation by the author.

[16] Paloma Valencia, interview by author, Online, 09/05/2023.

[17] Iván Duque, interview by author, Oxford, 02/07/2024.

[18] Wilson Ortiz, interview.

Congress and other elective institutions, as no sanction had been issued against them.

Criticism of the JEP's effectiveness comes not only from opponents of the Peace Agreement, but also from its supporters. In February 2024, all the members of the last Secretariat of the FARC-EP condemned the lack of definitive rulings as a proof that the JEP was going astray from its original purpose, as I will extensively explain below. For now, it is relevant to point out the specific critiques their party made to the JEP's ineffectiveness and operation costs. On April 18, 2024, *Comunes* described in an extensive thread on X that, according to a response to a freedom of information request they made, the JEP had not substituted any penal sanction to any agent of the conflict, nor had it waived the right to prosecute of non-most responsible, nor had it sanctioned any "most responsible". They claimed that "what we are asking is that those responsible are sanctioned soon because they have already acknowledged their responsibility. We ask the honouring of the letter and spirit of the Peace Agreement" (Partido COMUNES [@ComunesCoL] 2024). They argued that the JEP was conceived as a closure tribunal, where the main actors of the internal armed conflict would appear to satisfy victims' rights to truth and justice. Yet, they claimed, the JEP had become "a Tribunal that only adjudicates and investigates those who were insurgents and the middle ranks of the Army" (Partido COMUNES [@ComunesCoL] 2024). They also stated that from its creation until December 31, 2023, the JEP's budget had reached 2 trillion pesos, which they considered a large sum of money. In other words, the most salient representatives of the FARC-EP and their party, Comunes, have begun to claim that the JEP was going astray from what they had signed, and one of those reasons is that the JEP has been ineffective in offering legal certainty to the *comparecientes* and in adjudicating the crimes of all parties involved. This is relevant because, until then, former members of the FARC-EP had been among the JEP's most consistent defenders; however, dissatisfaction with the JEP's rulings and delays changed their perspective.

Internally, some JEP justices are aware that issuing definitive decisions in a reasonable time frame is essential to maintain the JEP's legitimacy. One justice of the Appellate Section,[19] the JEP's apex section, confirmed that promptness is essential to the JEP's legitimacy. Two justices at the

[19] Interviewee 17, interview by author, Bogotá, 08/14/2023.

SRVR agreed on that note and explained that, in their experience, the workload has not been effectively distributed[20]: the Panels have been executing the main functions of the JEP and their personnel is less qualified and less numerous than that of the less busy Higher Sections, as described 3.5. This workload ineffective distribution was also observed by Sebastián Escobar, victims' attorney,[21] who stressed that the SRVR had so many functions that it even had to make a proposal of the *sanciones propias*.

On the whole, the perception that the JEP is not meeting the essential goals of satisfying the victims' right to justice and the *comparecientes'* right to legal certainty is increasing. Whatever the cause, a slow pace in delivering definitive outcomes decisions has been increasingly prompting social dissatisfaction. Opponents, victims and even the ex-FARC-EP, who previously defended the JEP, are unsatisfied with the lack of definitive decisions. The JEP might come to be perceived as an expensive inefficient Tribunal, and that might elicit discussions to change or eliminate the JEP. Ineffectiveness might curtail the JEP's diffuse support. This example shows how, in the JEP's case, specific support might be connected to diffuse support in the medium term, as Sandra Botero suggested, in opposition to the main argument of literature (2020).

5.2.4 *Framing of the JEP's Decisions*

Following what was stated in the conceptual framework, Forero-Alba and Rodríguez-Raga posited that Courts that framed decisions in legal and scientific arguments have more legitimacy and are more trustworthy (2022, 190). Similarly, the JEP usually seeks to frame its written decisions in legal arguments, using its legal sources—national and international criminal law. But the institution also tries to frame its decisions in restorative terms, especially during the ARVR. Furthermore, as Gonzalo Sánchez,[22] director of the National Centre for Historical Memory between 2011 and 2018, stated:

[20] Interviewee 16, interview by author, Oxford, 10/03/2024; interviewee 11, interview by author, Bogotá, 08/30/2023.

[21] Escobar, interview.

[22] Gonzalo Sánchez, interview by author, Bogotá, 07/25/2023.

> The lack of sentences was compensated with public presentations of the perpetrators, their confessions, their responsibilities and their interpellations, [...] In a hearing, many things come into play: once these hearings are presented, there are the judges, there are the victims, there are the parties' attorneys, but there is also a society that listens and observes, and is making judgments. Above the JEP, it is society itself that is making judgments about the process.[23]

Sánchez points out the importance of public hearings to offset the lack of definitive rulings and to prompt judgements in society. In other words, this is an opportunity for the JEP to frame its rulings and showcase its processes. As I directly confirmed in the Yopal ARVR and as a digital spectator of the ARVR of the last Secretariat of the FARC-EP in June 2022 and that of Ocaña in July 2022, rulings accepting or rejecting the *comparecientes*' acknowledgement of truth and responsibility of the indicted crimes are framed as a result of a thorough restorative process.

This process consists of many preparatory sessions of psychosocial attention to victims and *comparecientes*, among them, private sessions prior to the hearing where both parties dialogue and perpetrators respond to the victims' claims. In the public hearing, *comparecientes* manifest their responsibility for the crimes, acknowledge the judicial truth of the facts, a substantial number of them show remorse, and offer some restorative actions towards the victims.

One notable example of restorative actions is the one that occurred during the Yopal ARVR in September 2023. First, Mayor Gustavo Enrique Soto Bracamonte lit a large candle in front of the victims, in memory of their loved ones. Then, Captain Jaime Rivera handed to the JEP the medal he had achieved thanks to the "*falsos positivos*" he reported. The scene was framed within several painted vases, which the victims had restored honouring their loved ones. As part of the JEP's psychosocial attention, the victims painted them as a symbol of the restoration of

[23] Quote in Spanish: "El déficit de sentencias fue compensado con los procesos de puesta en escena pública de los responsables, de sus confesiones, de sus responsabilidades y de sus interpelaciones, [...] que no son solamente de la institucionalidad, sino, en una audiencia, entran muchas cosas en juego: una vez que se pone en escena una de estas audiencias, están los jueces, están las víctimas, están los abogados de las partes, pero está la sociedad que escucha y observa, y está emitiendo juicios. La sociedad, antes que la JEP, es la propia sociedad la que está emitiendo juicios sobre el proceso mismo."

their dignity and as a means to process their grief. This is visible in the Image 5.1.

These symbols, dialogues and interactions build a narrative that is difficult to refute. As Santiago Rodríguez[24] suggests, the connection between the victims' and the perpetrators' versions demolishes any effort from the JEP's opponents to deny such truth. This effect was thoroughly explained by Roberto Vidal, the, President of the JEP, as of September 2023[25]:

> In a public hearing [...] the victims' truth, confirmed by the *comparecientes*' confession, produces an irrefutable level of truth in society... so those who had been in permanent denial about certain issues (*falsos positivos*) give in. When you face the "argumentative wall" [provided by] some victims, placed in a position of political dignity, in front of some *comparecientes* who acknowledge this, when you bring these two things together, we ask ourselves: what can the judge say to that? Who could say anything to that? Not even the most opposed political sectors, nor the most powerful ones; they all surrender before this truth, and so does the judge. Can you imagine a judge saying: "I do not accept this truth"?[26]

The confirmation of the victims' truth by the perpetrators builds an "argumentative wall", which is very difficult to deny. Hearings become framing spaces to reinforce and dignify the victims' truth.

For example, after the Dabeiba ARVR, former President Álvaro Úribe Vélez, in office at the time when most of the "*falsos positivos*" were perpetrated, had to accept the existence of such crimes, after denying them for more than a decade. He claimed that members of the Armed Forces lied to him, that such crimes tainted his security policy, and that "any

[24] Rodríguez, interview.

[25] Roberto Vidal, interview by author, Bogotá, 08/09/2023.

[26] Quote in Spanish: "En una audiencia pública [...] la verdad de las víctimas, confirmada por la confesión de los comparecientes, produce un nivel de verdad irrefutable en la sociedad, que mira que sectores que habían hecho negación permanente de algunas cuestiones (falsos positivos) [ceden]. Cuando tú te enfrentas con la pared argumentativa de unas víctimas, puestas en un lugar de dignificación política, frente a unos comparecientes que reconocen eso, cuando cruzas esas dos cosas, nosotros nos preguntamos: ¿y el juez qué puede decirle a esto? ¿es que quién le puede decir algo a eso? Ni los sectores políticos más opuestos, ni los más poderosos, todos se rinden ante esta verdad, pero también el juez. Tú te imaginas al juez diciendo: '¿yo no admito esa verdad?'".

of these crimes is serious regardless of their number or the cases of false accusations" (Álvaro Uribe Vélez [@AlvaroUribeVel] 2023).

In Gustavo Salazar's and Alejandro Ramelli's opinions, both JEP justices and respective coordinators of the case of Unión Patriótica and Dabeiba, this hearing also changed the narrative of *falsos positivos*.[27] The latter, coordinator of the hearing, affirmed that threats and attacks against himself and his teams were significantly reduced after the hearing.

Furthermore, in these scenarios, some victims, even if they do not participate directly in the hearings, might feel represented. Since the JEP will address general patterns of victimisation and not all the specific cases of the internal armed conflict, as was explained in the Introduction and Historical Background chapters, hearings become symbols where the victims and non-victims could relate to the stories and restorative processes presented.

5.2.5 *Equal Treatment in Investigating, Adjudicating and Sanctioning Members of the FARC-EP and the Armed Forces*

In other contexts, the treatment of Armed Forces and guerrilla members has not been a central issue. In some cases, crimes committed by one party were not adjudicated at all. For instance, in the agreement between the government and the M-19 (1990), the guerrilla was granted a full amnesty, whereas some of the Armed Forces members were held accountable for their crimes. In Argentina, members of the military junta faced prosecution in court (1985), while investigations into the crimes committed by former members of the guerrilla "Montoneros" were less common.

In other countries, Armed Forces members have avoided accountability. For example, in Northern Ireland, criminal cases related to excessive force in counter-terrorist actions have generally failed, as Juliana Van Hoeven has described (2016). The extent of the UK Government's involvement in the violence is still unclear, leading many scholars in the decade of 2000s to call for the implementation of transitional justice mechanisms to clarify the events of "The Troubles" (Connolly 2006; Hamber 2002).

[27] Salazar, interview. Ramelli, interview.

In contrast, the satisfaction with the JEP's decisions partly hinges on treating equally the FARC-EP and the Armed Forces. For Rodrigo Londoño,[28] before known as "Timochenko", the last chief commander of the FARC-EP, this is essential to avoid "trading blame"—prosecuting only one party of the internal armed conflict. On the other political side, Álvaro Uribe Vélez has consistently argued that the JEP treats the Armed Forces like terrorists such as the FARC-EP. Similarly, Paloma Valencia[29] claimed that Armed Forces members should have a special Panel with expert judges in International Humanitarian Law. For the first, equality is a sign that the JEP is fair; for the latter, it is proof that it is skewed.

The legislation and the operation of the JEP were designed to address these tensions. In a negotiated transition like Colombia's—where the national government and the FARC-EP agreed on the terms for finishing the war and adjudicating related crimes—symmetry in treatment fosters trust among the parties. It reassures all actors that the judicial system will not be used against them. Legally, Armed Forces agents have a guarantee that they would have the same treatment as the former FARC-EP combatants. For example, if they are not identified as "most responsible", both former *guerrilleros* and State agents can request that the JEP waive prosecution of their crimes, once they fulfilling a regime of conditionalities aimed at satisfying victims' rights.

In its operation, the JEP has also tried to equally investigate and prosecute the Armed Forces and the FARC-EP. As stated in the previous chapter, the SRVR opened three cases exclusively related to the FARC-EP, three related to the State forces or public authorities, and five cases involving both parties. The first ARVR against FARC-EP and Armed Forces were held only two months apart: the first hearing on "*falsos positivos*" was in April 2022 and the one on kidnappings by the FARC-EP in June 2022.

5.2.6 *Acceptance of Restorative Justice*

Restorative justice is one of the most controversial elements of the JEP. As victims' attorney Sebastián Escobar[30] pointed out, it entails a remarkable

[28] Rodrigo Londoño Echeverri, interview by author, Bogotá, 08/16/2023.

[29] Valencia, interview.

[30] Escobar, interview.

change from Colombia's traditional punitive paradigm. Until the signing of the Peace Agreement, Colombia had had a retributive justice that mostly sanctioned crimes with jail, associating punishment with suffering. In Colombian society, it is common to hear the expression: "*que se pudran en la cárcel*" ("may the rot in prison"). In contrast, the JEP prioritises restorative justice. As described in the previous section, that approach entails a dialogue between the parties throughout processes clarifying the truth, providing restorative measures and dignifying the victims. When these conditions are met, the JEP imposes more lenient sanctions that do not involve imprisonment.

Certainly, this new paradigm clashes with the retributive one and may seem unfair and disproportional to the crimes committed. Therefore, the acceptance or resistance to restorative justice in the JEP impacts societal satisfaction with the JEP's rulings. The more people accept restorative justice concrete cases, the more they will support the JEP's decisions, and vice versa.

In fact, the most recent survey of the Americas Barometer shows that, in 2023, most people (57%) were neither in favour nor against the fact that those responsible for war-related crimes are punished with sentences that do not involve imprisonment, provided that they confess their actions and contribute to clarifying the truth (Rodríguez-Raga 2023, 51–53).

However, respondents reacted differently to a concrete case of restorative justice. In the hypothetical case where the soldier Carlos Soto confessed a murder and received a more lenient sentence of house arrest and clearing landmines, 51% of respondents were against it—those who expressed support from 1 to 3. Those who had a neutral perception were 33%—reporting support from 4 to 5—and supporters of restorative cases were only 16%. Therefore, it seems that Colombians neither support nor refuse the idea of restorative justice, but most reject a case of it when it is applied and many have a neutral opinion on this issue. This trend shows that the JEP is still finding resistance to the idea of restorative justice (Image 5.4).

The acceptance of restorative justice requires that the JEP convinces the citizens that restorative justice is fair—being proportional to the crimes—and valid for punishing them. Several interviewees discussed this challenge. María Isabel Ortiz,[31] the journalist that by 2023 covered the

[31] María Isabel Ortiz, interview by author, Bogotá, 09/06/2023.

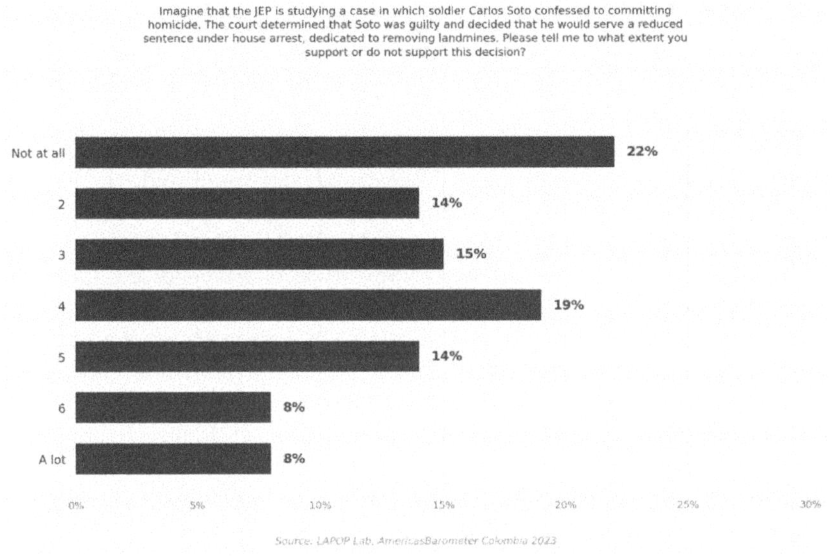

Image 5.4 Support for a concrete restorative justice case in the JEP (*Source* Graph by the author, based on Rodríguez-Raga [2023])

JEP for *El Tiempo*—the most read newspaper in Colombia—said that "restorative justice is a thought sell". Similarly, an international organisation member that supports the JEP pointed out that the social knowledge of *sanciones propias* is a pedagogical challenge.

Gonzalo Sánchez,[32] who worked since its origin and for over a decade in the National Centre for Historical Memory, observed that institutions "do not sell themselves". He then asked himself: "what is the JEP's narrative?" ("*¿cuál es la narrativa de la JEP?*").[33] This means that the JEP must actively seek the acceptance of restorative justice. Its existence per se does not entail prestige or the acceptance of its rulings. In its operation, the JEP must build a narrative to convince society that restorative justice is an effective justice, as Sebastián Escobar stated.[34]

[32] Gonzalo Sánchez, interview by author, Bogotá, 07/25/2023.

[33] Original quote: ¿cuál es la narrativa de la JEP? Translated by the author.

[34] Escobar, interview.

The JEP's authority hinges partly on the acceptance of society—and especially of the victims. The institution must convince its audience of the pertinence of restorative justice to overcome the crimes committed in the internal armed conflict.

Some advantages of the restorative justice approach have begun to become visible in the hearings. As Roberto Vidal suggested, the combination of the versions of the victims and the guerrilleros constitutes a "truth wall" difficult to break or contradict. But it is still uncertain how the restorative actions would work. Seven years have passed since the JEP's creation, but the JEP has not showcased a clear example of *sanciones propias*, at most, in April 2024, the system of restorative actions started to work in Bogotá (El País 2024). In the project *Siembras de Vida*, those deemed as most responsible for *falsos positivos*, like Gustavo Soto Bracamonte, will plant trees to restore the forest around Usme, an area that was heavily affected by the internal armed conflict. The JEP coordinated this project after receiving many suggestions from victims' organisations and *comparecientes*. Previously, the *comparecientes* had voluntarily carried out *Trabajos, Obras o Actividades con contenido Reparador o Restaurativo* (TOAR)—restorative works or activities. For instance, by 2020, former members of the FARC-EP had participated in a demining project at Briceño (Antioquia) and at Mesetas (Meta). They had also conducted a botanical expedition at Anorí (Antioquia) (JEP Press Office 2020). These TOAR were carried out voluntarily by the *comparecientes* as an anticipated element of the sanctions. But *Siembras de Vida* has been the first project implemented by the JEP.

Some interviewees were mindful that the JEP should persuade society that restorative justice is fair and is not impunity. For instance, Óscar Parra underlined the importance of framing the rulings to convince that they are proportional to the crimes committed.[35] He and Ariel Sánchez, then director of the JEP Restorative Justice Department, as for August 2023,[36] stressed that restorative justice is not only about the sanctions but also about the process. Interested sectors, like victims and society in general, may find more satisfaction in observing the *comparecientes* genuinely ask for forgiveness, show remorse and effectively compromise with the non-recurrence of the crimes, than seeing them in jail. Only

[35] Parra, interview.

[36] Ariel Sánchez, interview by author, Bogotá, 08/03/2023.

putting into place restorative justice and showing these processes might foster or undermine the acceptance of restorative justice. Paraphrasing Gonzalo Sanchez's idea—"institutions do not sell themselves"—restorative justice does not sell itself. It is necessary to convince society about its effectiveness.

5.2.7 *Salient Cases of Dissatisfaction with the JEP's Rulings: The Claim of the Last FARC-EP Secretariat That the JEP Derailed*

As documented in this book, the JEP has had strong opponents, especially from the right. But in February 2024 salient figures of the former FARC-EP, among them Rodrigo Londoño Echeverry, the ex-top commander of the FARC, have also argued that the JEP "*se descarriló*" ("derailed"). This opposition is not minor. It shows a substantial dissatisfaction of one party of the Peace Agreement with the JEP's rulings, impacting diffuse support.

In February 2024, the only seven living members of the Secretariat of the FARC-EP (its top structure of command) asked President Petro for a meeting to discuss that the JEP was going astray from the original design they agreed upon. In their opinion, the JEP was breaking the Peace Agreement, and, as a result, they suggested the creation of another Tribunal of closure, one that would include all the actors of violence in Colombia. The former commanders also said that they would be forced not to comply with any ruling if the JEP kept operating as it did. Furthermore, they implied that many of the rank-and-file members had been forced to join the existing organised armed groups, facing the judicial insecurity caused by the delays of the institution (La Silla Vacía [@lasillavacia] 2024).

The former FARC-EP secretariat's complaints were essentially based on four arguments. First, the amnesties guerilla members were supposed to benefit from had not been granted or were taking a long time to be processed. Out of 4,485 requested amnesties, only 688 were granted. The rest were denied, breaching the Article 6.5 of the Protocol II to the Geneva Conventions, according to which States should offer "the widest amnesty possible" to combatants, after an armed conflict. As a result, former guerrilleros lived in a situation of judicial insecurity, distrusted the JEP and had difficulties reincorporating into the civilian life. Second, as combatants of the medium ranks were being investigated in case one, among others, the JEP was unnecessarily deviating from its original task of clarifying representative cases. Third, in their opinion, the concept of "manifest desertion"—when the JEP promptly expels individuals from its jurisdiction, after confirming that they have taken up the arms again by a strikingly evident proof, like it did with "Santrich"—was a violation to the right of due process. Fourth, the JEP's intention of handing down several "*resolución de conclusiones*", instead of a unique one, dishonoured the Peace Agreement and the principle of legality. In a few words, this means that the FARC-EP members could face many sanctions corresponding to as many "*resolución de conclusiones*" as they would get indicted for, instead of serving only one sanction for the only "*resolución de conclusiones*" concerning all the crimes they claim they had agreed upon.

Unsurprisingly, the letter prompted an intense reaction among the JEP, intellectuals and even the victims. A couple of days after the letter was published, the JEP issued a press release that stressed that any submitted individual should comply with the JEP's rulings, and those who refrained from doing so would lose their benefits and their cases would be resumed in the ordinary Tribunals (Semana 2024a).

Weeks later, the JEP organised an event to inaugurate a digital platform that collects all the granted amnesties, regardless of whether they were decided by the Government, the ordinary jurisdiction or the JEP. This unified database would foster judicial certainty among the former members of the FARC-EP, who would know if they have been granted an amnesty. Yet, in his speech on the day of the event, Rodrigo Londoño Echeverri "Timochenko" insisted that their cases should be definitively resolved (2024).

Once the letter drafted by the FARC was published, Roberto Vidal, the president of the JEP and spokesperson, defended the JEP's work in several interviews (Semana 2024b). He mentioned that the FARC-EP's claims were politically motivated and, since the JEP was a judicial institution, it would not respond for political actions; it would only operate in judicial terms. He added that the former members of the FARC-EP had legal actions to contest the judicial decisions and the JEP would duly process them, guaranteeing independence, justice and balance. Lastly, he specified that the unresolved amnesties were complex to decide, due to the particularities of each case and emphatically rejected the idea of another Tribunal of closure.

Alluding to the letter, Yesid Reyes, one of the designers of the JEP appointed by former President Santos, pointed out that the JEP had been misinterpreting the rules of their Statutes (2024). It had been clarifying many cases, providing as much truth as possible but, in his opinion, that was not its initial purpose. The Truth Commission was in charge of explaining the truth of what happened in the internal armed conflict, whereas the JEP had to adjudicate and sanction the "most responsible" of that conflict. Thus, the Truth Commission was maximalist, while the JEP was essentially minimalist. By seeking to expand its scope, the JEP would get distracted from its main purpose and might not accomplish it. So, he recommended opening the dialogue to find a common interpretation of the Peace Agreement, aiming to find consensus on the JEP's operation.

Paola Molano acknowledged that the former members of the FARC-EP were partially right, but they were still bound to fulfil the JEP's ruling as one of the parties of the Peace Agreement (2024a). She mentioned that the JEP's delays in handing down rulings were unjustified: it had not decided a single sentence neither for the FARC-EP former combatants, nor the agents of the Armed Forces. In her opinion, Vidal's position was unacceptable in that he should point out when the definitive rulings were going to be decided. This would mean meeting the main objective of the JEP and fulfilling the victims' expectations. Transitions are a window of opportunity, and as time passes, the outcomes of a transitional justice mechanism progressively lose their relevance.

Not only intellectuals and interested individuals discussed this controversy. On their side, some of the FARC-EP victims who participate in the JEP's proceedings increasingly asked the FARC-EP to comply with the rulings. They also recognise the importance of the JEP's work and the positive results of the proceedings (El Espectador 2024).

As can be observed, the delays in handing down definitive rulings, the thoroughness with which the JEP has been doing its job, and its intention of issuing several sentences according to the crimes the FARC-EP members committed have been causing discontent within the FARC-EP. In turn, the former commanders have been testing the political support of finding an alternative Tribunal for the accountability of their crimes; they have suggested refraining from recognising the rulings of the JEP. Some experts on the JEP, like Yesid Reyes and Paola Molano, have also pointed out the slowness of the JEP's proceedings, while the JEP defends its job. However, it seems that its legitimacy begins to be contested by the top commanders of the FARC-EP. Thus, specific support can affect the diffuse support of an essential actor, salient members of the FARC-EP who argue that they speak as signatories of the Peace Agreement.

5.3 Discussion Between Specific Support and Diffuse Support

The recent critiques from the last FARC-EP Secretariat prompt a question relevant to the academic literature: to what extent does the satisfaction with the decisions of the JEP, or the lack of decisions affect diffuse support? This question is important because, according to Easton, specific and diffuse supports are completely disconnected in older, established courts (1975). Diffuse support offsets the negative effects of an unpopular decision.

Drawing on these concepts, Gibson et al. posited that, in recently established institutions, diffuse support could be low when specific support is high because Courts have not had enough time to build a "goodwill reservoir" (1998, 344). Furthermore, the relation between diffuse and specific support is strongly associated with "whether people already have established attitudes toward the institution or whether the institution is relatively unknown" (Gibson et al. 1998, 345). At the same time, only consistent dissatisfaction can undermine the levels of diffuse support, even if these levels are scarce. In 2020, Botero pointed out that, as any new Court, the JEP lacks a goodwill reservoir and, as any transitional justice mechanism, it addresses controversial and unpopular topics. As a result, "we might expect that, over the medium term, specific rulings could negatively influence institutional support for this court" (2020, 303).

In other words, the JEP was created with a goodwill reservoir deeply related to the "established attitudes towards the institution", that is, mostly, the support or rejection of the 2016 Peace Agreement. Over time, the JEP has been able to build a reservoir on its own by crystallising the satisfaction or dissatisfaction with its rulings, hearings, symbols and ceremonies. Yet, in the medium term, prolonged dissatisfaction with the JEP's rulings might erode diffuse support because the JEP might be perceived as an ineffective institution.

In fact, according to Shany, the effectiveness of an organisation can be measured by identifying: (1) the organisation's goals, (2) the desired outcome and (3) "the time frame over which it is reasonable to expect that some or all of these goals could be met" (2014, 14). Thus, in the JEP's case, the goals are "satisfying the victims' right to justice, providing truth to the Colombian society, protecting the victims' rights, contributing to achieving a stable and lasting peace, and taking decisions that ensure judicial certainty to those who participated in grave human rights violations" (Congress of the Republic of Colombia 2017). The desired outcome is that those goals are met; the time frame to fulfil them is initially ten years, which can be extended two times by five years, for a total of 20 years. However, it is reasonable to expect that the JEP's objectives might be achieved to some extent at this point, after six years of operation have passed.

According to the 2023 Americas Barometer reports' findings, only 29% of the respondents stated that the JEP had satisfied the victims' rights to truth, reparation and justice (Rodríguez-Raga 2023, 53). In contrast, 49% of the respondents said that the JEP had failed to meet those goals, while 23% said that the JEP had achieved those goals to some extent. In a few words, only a minority of the respondents thinks that the JEP has satisfied the victims' rights, whereas a vast majority is either sceptical about this work or claims that it has not achieved it whatsoever.

As discussed above, the JEP has been able to provide truth to Colombian society to some extent, through the macro-cases and the ARVR, while protecting the victims' rights and contributing to build a stable and lasting peace. The delays in handing down definitive rulings call into question its capacity to meet two of its main goals: (1) providing justice to victims and (2) guaranteeing legal certainty to the *comparecientes*. In sum, the JEP's ineffectiveness in provide justice and guarantee legal certainty erodes specific support because it creates dissatisfaction with the scarcity of rulings on these fronts, and when such dissatisfaction persists, it undermines diffuse support, as the FARC-EP's case shows.

At least three of the interviewees who worked in the JEP were mindful of this. In their view, they all claimed that the JEP's legitimacy hinges on its rulings and, most of all, on "getting the work done".[37] One of them boldly argued that those who get the work done are hard to get rid of. Conversely, those who do not get their job done are easily eradicated. At the time of the interviews, this was a major concern among the JEP interviewees: five years had passed out of the ten of initial duration, and it did not seem likely that the JEP was going to finalise its operation in such a period. Some interviewees were in favour of asking for a mandate extension, others were against it. Be it as it may, a little over seven months after

[37] Interviewee 17, interview by author. Bogotá, 08/14/2023. Interviewee 9, interview by author. Bogotá, 07/26/2023. Interviewee 20, interview by author. 08/25/2023.

the interviews, the last FARC-EP Secretariat published its letter strongly criticising the JEP's lack of definitive rulings.

Other interviewees expressed their concerns about the extent to which the JEP's rulings were able to guarantee the non-recurrence of the crimes and contribute to the Colombian transition. For example, Eduardo Pizarro Leóngomez,[38] a scholar expert on transitions, underlined that the JEP's context is very particular: citing the title of a book by Rodrigo Uprimny et al. (2006), the JEP's was a case of "transitional justice without transition" ("*justicia transicional sin transición*"). This entails challenges because the JEP operation might disappoint the societal expectations, when not curbed to the particular scenario. Unlike the Argentine case, where a Tribunal adjudicated the cases after the dictatorship had ended, the JEP is adjudicating crimes while the Colombian internal armed conflict is still happening.

It could be argued that the FARC-EP demobilised and the JEP is contributing to that transition. But even in those cases, "Jesús Santrich" and "Iván Márquez", among others, who were signatories of the Peace Agreement, later became deserters and founded a new armed group—the "Segunda Marquetalia"—arguing that the State had betrayed them.

As explained above, the JEP ruled in favour of "Jesús Santrich", after which he became a deserter. Some people might perceive this decision as a proof that the JEP has not been helping to contribute to the Colombian transition, which might put the JEP's ability to contribute to the transition in doubt.

In conclusion, in the JEP's case, dissatisfaction with rulings or the lack of definitive decisions might affect societal loyalty to the JEP in the medium term. Unlike ordinary high courts, the JEP has a limited time of existence where it is expected to accomplish its objectives—guaranteeing the victims' rights to justice, truth, reparation and non-recurrence; providing legal certainty to the *comparecientes*; and establishing judicial truth for the Colombian society. If it is perceived that during the period of existence, the JEP has not been able to accomplish those goals, the diffuse support for it might decrease, as happened in the case of the extinct FARC-EP.

[38] Eduardo Pizarro Leóngomez, interview by author, Bogotá, 07/10/2023.

5.4 Salience

The Americas Barometer 2023 report established that less than 1 out of 3 Colombians understood how the JEP works (29%), after asking the respondents to self-report the extent to which they knew the way the JEP operates. Although it could be large challenge, doing pedagogy about the JEP's operation might be of use: the same report describes that the proportion of those who trust in the JEP doubles among those who know how it works compared to those that ignore it. This could explain the JEP's communicative efforts.

For being a young Court, the JEP is salient. It deals with controversial issues, the media has extensive coverage of the JEP's operations, many of its most important hearings have been televised, and all of them are broadcast through YouTube. As a result, in a short period for a Court, the JEP has exposed Colombian society to its legitimising symbols, some of which have been explained above in Sect. 5.2.4.

Unlike other Colombian Courts, the JEP has been executing a communication strategy through many means, as Hernando Salazar, then Director of Communications at the JEP, pointed out.[39] The JEP has extensive interaction on Twitter and Facebook, it has been one of the first Colombian Courts to use TikTok, and the only one that records all its hearings on YouTube. It also has a podcast and a radio programme "*Por fin lo sabemos*" / "Finally we know it", produced by Radio Nacional Colombia, the public radio company. Communication is perceived by several JEP law clerks, administrative employees and justices as a pedagogical space to teach about the institution's design.

Yet, the fact that the JEP might achieve some salience does not mean that its role, decisions and proceedings are understood, validated and attractive. Santiago Rodríguez[40] and María Isabel Ortiz,[41] who respectively covered the JEP for La Silla Vacía and El Tiempo, describe this fact in terms like "*la paz no es sexy*" ("peace is not sexy"), "*la paz no es lo más taquillero*" ("Peace is not the most viral topic"). News explaining the JEP's symbols is less read than political scandals. In other words, social groups might be exposed to legitimising symbols but that does not mean they will become interested in the JEP's operation. Citizens could react

[39] Hernando Salazar, interview by author, Bogotá, 08/11/2023.

[40] Rodríguez, interview.

[41] Ortiz, interview.

with disinterest to the JEP's rulings and hearings. They might also not fully understand the sui-generis mixed approach of restorative and retributive justice. This reinforces the need for the JEP to explain its operation, symbols and structure by different means (radio, podcast, press releases, video). It has been doing so, even consistently participating in Bogota's book fair. However, the effectiveness of these measures is still unclear.

Furthermore, it is possible that the fact that the JEP remains outside the scandals could feed its legitimacy. It takes time to build reputation, and corruption and scandals can easily damage its reputation.

5.5 Obedience

In general, the JEP decisions have been enforced. The best example of the JEP judicial authority is the compliance of the "Santrich" decision. It imposed a significant challenge due to pressure from the US Justice Department and the resignation of the Attorney General. Yet, the ruling was complied with, and "Santrich" was released from jail.

In other cases, the JEP has ordered house arrest for the public servants in charge of implementing measures to protect cemeteries that could contain disappeared people's remains. In December 2023, the Governor of the Department of Valle del Cauca, Clara Luz Roldán, complied with two days of house arrest for not honouring the compromises to protect areas where the JEP could potentially find remains of disappeared people. Neither she nor anyone from her government attended the hearings at the allocated time to intervene regarding this issue. As she was complying the decision, she strongly criticised it:

> I want to announce that tomorrow I will comply with the ruling handed down by the JEP. What an irony, how many criminals are free because they are submitted to the JEP's jurisdiction, appointed as peace agents, without a day in prison or reparation to their victims. (Semana 2023a)[42]

Similarly, in June 2023, Robinson Manosalva, major of the municipality of Aguachica, served two days of house arrest for failing to

[42] Original quote: "Quiero anunciar que el día de mañana cumpliré el fallo proferido por la JEP. Qué ironía, cuánto criminal libre porque se acoge a la JEP, nombrados gestores de paz, sin un día de cárcel ni reparación a sus víctimas". Translation by the author.

safeguard the *Cementerio de los Pobres* of his town (Semana 2023b). As a sign of protest, he posted a video using strong vocabulary:

> They [the JEP's justices] are stupid, [to go to jail] that's what criminals, bandits, corrupt people are for. It is a thing to order a precautionary measure against me for not digging up some bastards who have been buried for 50 years, who are dead, who have families, by order of some guerrilla fucks called justices.[43]

After this message, the JEP ordered the criminal and administrative investigation of Manosalva for insulting the victims and the justices. The tone of both messages, but especially the last one, indicates that disobedience of the JEP's rulings is used as a political means to defy the JEP's social authority and ultimately the idea of peace it symbolises. In short, although in general the rulings are complied with, the existence of cases as the ones I pointed out means that the JEP social legitimacy might be at stake daily. Politicians could disobey the JEP's rulings to activate emotional devices against what the JEP might symbolise in their discourse: impunity, biased decisions in favour of *guerrilleros*, unreasonable liberty for criminals without proper reparation to the victims. The JEP could be weaponised to convey criticism for the peace process and support for stronger measures against former members of the FARC-EP.

5.6 Age

Age and time are essential elements to the JEP. The JEP is a recent Court with a limited time of existence for accomplishing its goals. Therefore, as the institution has recognised it under the principle of "strict temporality", the JEP must be effective. In the initial stages, it did not have a goodwill reservoir to rely on. Societal perception came from the support or rejection for the Peace Agreement. Furthermore, as victims' attorney Sebastián Escobar suggested,[44] the JEP did not have the burden of impunity of ordinary tribunals.

[43] Original quote: "Son como maricas, para esto están los delincuentes, los bandidos, los corruptos, una cosa es que me den una medida cautelar por no desenterrar un poco de huevones que tienen más de 50 años de estar enterrados, muertos, que tienen familia, por orden de unos hp guerrilleros llamados magistrados".

[44] Escobar, interview.

As time has passed, Colombian society has been able to do a running tally of the transitional justice decisions. Based on that, perceptions have changed. Most of the interviewees agreed that the JEP has increased its sociological legitimacy over time, and some argued that the Petro administration has been a period where the JEP has financial support to increase its staff and operations. Time is also limited for a transitional justice system. Hence, the older a transitional justice tribunal, the greater the expectations of accomplishing its goals. Contrary to the existing literature, in the JEP's case, as times passes, the decisions might increasingly affect the societal loyalty, especially if they are definitive. Certainly, the upcoming imposition of *sanciones propias* will be a landmark moment that will test the JEP's sociological legitimacy. As Paola Molano tweeted:

> Let us not forget that the JEP exists as a function of the transition, not as an end in itself. So the longer it goes on, the less relevant its results are to society, because transition is a tiny window of opportunity that is progressively closing. (Paola Molano Ayala [@pmolanoayala] 2024b)[45]

As the JEP becomes older, its outcomes might become less relevant, given that transitions are windows of opportunity. As times passes, society expects more positive effects from the decisions taken in the past; it expects signs of the transition. This case is interesting because the JEP's performance might affect its age. If it does not deliver properly, it might not get an extension. Ultimately, its existence hinges on its proper operation.

5.7 Scale

Having described the JEP legitimacy factors, it is important to estimate them in the scale I previously proposed Sect. 4.2.5. Diffuse support is high because, over time, most individuals have not been willing to make fundamental changes to the JEP, and contentious decisions are accepted.

[45] Original quote: ""No se nos olvide que la JEP existe en función de la transición, no como un fin en sí misma. Así que entre más tiempo pase, sus resultados son menos relevantes ante la sociedad, pues la transición es una ventana de oportunidad chiquita que se está cerrando progresivamente."

The Constitutional Court and Congress, as well as international organisations like the ICC and the UN Security Council, have supported the JEP. Individuals somewhat trust in the JEP.

In terms of specific support, some social groups have expressed major critiques—the FARC-EP, the *uribismo*. The latter did so in the initial years and lately it has been less vocal, even accepting the existence of *falsos positivos* and deflecting the responsibility to those members of the Armed Forces who committed the crimes. The first have criticised the lack of definitive rulings of *sanciones propias*, amnesties and a unique indictment. Victims have expressed minor concerns especially regarding their participation, although there has not been a massive drop out of the JEP's proceedings.

In absence of definitive rulings, hearings have become the landmark spaces to frame the JEP's outcomes, to explain their logic and to educate the population about the ideas of restorative justice. The JEP has been trying to treat and prosecute both the FARC-EP and the Armed Forces equally. The idea of restorative justice is somewhat accepted, but, according to polls, it is more refused when it is applied to a concrete case. This highlights that the JEP's framing of *sanciones propias*, the application of restorative justice to specific scenarios, is going to be essential to the acceptance of restorative justice.

In short, most social groups are somewhat satisfied with the JEP's outcomes, while some have major critiques, and restorative justice is somewhat accepted. Therefore, specific support is medium and might tend to pass to low, depending on the speed in handing down definitive rulings and the framing of *sanciones propias* and other restorative actions.

As for obedience, in general, the JEP's rulings are complied with, even when they are held against someone who disobeyed a previous order. Yet, as I showed with some examples, there are cases of disobedience and critiques to the JEP that could be used as emotional devices to justify disobedience. As a result, obedience tends from medium to high.

Following Americas Barometer data, salience of the JEP is low. Less than 30% of Colombians understand the JEP's operation. However, given the media exposure and the cases the JEP adjudicates, it is possible that citizens know about the existence of the JEP but they might not understand its inner workings.

Taking into account the previous components, the JEP has a medium level of legitimacy that is explained by the levels of the different components of legitimacy. It could increase or decrease depending on the most pressing issues at the moment—the lack of salience and definitive rulings, the efficacy of the *sanciones propias*, the satisfaction of the victims regarding their participation and the major critiques coming from an essential actor (the top public figures of those who belonged to the FARC-EP). In other words, how the JEP deals with these pressing matters will directly contribute to the variation of its legitimacy.

References

Álvaro Uribe Vélez [@AlvaroUribeVel]. 2023. "Duele y mortifica que hubieran negado falsos positivos, les creímos, y ahora los aceptan; incluso la Fundación de Herbin Hoyos, qepd, defendió un caso de Dabeiba, anterior a mi Gbno. Y apoyamos esa defensa. Los cometidos durante mi Gbno mancharon la Seguridad Democrática que." Tweet. Twitter, June 29. https://twitter.com/AlvaroUribeVel/status/1674214007962583040.

Ámbito Jurídico. 2019. "Detalle de las razones de Duque al objetar la Ley Estatutaria de la JEP." Ámbito Jurídico, March 11. https://www.ambitojuridico.com/noticias/general/administrativo-y-contratacion/detalle-de-las-razones-de-duque-al-objetar-la-ley.

AP News. 2021. "Colombia: expresidente Uribe declara sobre falsos positivos." AP News, August 16. https://apnews.com/article/noticias-c2cf010e95c0e4836732aeab28a5da6d.

BBC News Mundo. 2019. "La Corte Constitucional de Colombia rechaza las objeciones de Duque a la polémica ley que juzga a los involucrados en el conflicto armado." *BBC News Mundo*, May 30. https://www.bbc.com/mundo/noticias-america-latina-48453600.

BBC News Mundo. 2021. "Las disidencias de las FARC confirman la muerte del guerrillero colombiano Jesús Santrich en territorio venezolano." *BBC News Mundo*, May 18. https://www.bbc.com/mundo/noticias-america-latina-57165018.

Botero, Sandra. 2020. Trust in Colombia's Justicia Especial Para La Paz: Experimental Evidence. *Journal of Politics in Latin America* 12 (3): 300–322. https://doi.org/10.1177/1866802X20959509.

Congress of the Republic of Colombia. 2017. "Constitutional Reform 1 of 2017." April 4. http://www.secretariasenado.gov.co/senado/basedoc/acto_legislativo_01_2017.html.

Connolly, Christopher K. 2006. Living on the Past: The Role of Truth Commissions in Post-Conflict Societies and the Case Study of Northern Ireland. *Cornell Int'l LJ* 39: 401.

Constitutional Court of Colombia. 2018. "Ruling C-080-18." August 15. https://www.corteconstitucional.gov.co/relatoria/2018/c-080-18.htm.

Easton, David. 1975. A Re-Assessment of the Concept of Political Support. *British Journal of Political Science* 5 (4): 435–457. https://doi.org/10.1017/S0007123400008309.

El Espectador. 2024. “El grito de respeto por la JEP que lideran las víctimas de las FARC.” Text. ELESPECTADOR.COM, March 10. https://www.elespectador.com/judicial/el-grito-de-respeto-por-la-jep-que-lideran-las-victimas-de-las-farc/.

El País. 2018. “La detención del exlíder de las FARC Jesús Santrich tensa el proceso de paz en Colombia.” América Colombia. *El País* (Madrid), April 11. https://elpais.com/internacional/2018/04/10/colombia/1523394661_758627.html.

El País. 2019. “El fiscal de Colombia dimite tras la orden de liberación de un exlíder de las FARC.” América Colombia. *El País* (Madrid), May 16. https://elpais.com/internacional/2019/05/15/colombia/1557944015_282644.html.

El País. 2024. “Comienza la justicia restaurativa en Colombia: los antiguos criminales de guerra que siembran bosques.” El País América Colombia, April 3. https://elpais.com/america-colombia/2024-04-03/comienza-la-justicia-restaurativa-en-colombia-los-antiguos-criminales-de-guerra-que-siembran-bosques.html.

Forero-Alba, Sofía, and Juan Carlos Rodríguez-Raga. 2022. “Courting Judicial Legitimacy: An Experimental Study of the Colombian Constitutional Court.” In *The Limits of Judicialization*, 1st ed., edited by Sandra Botero, Daniel M. Brinks, and Ezequiel A. Gonzalez-Ocantos. Cambridge University Press. https://doi.org/10.1017/9781009093859.007.

Gibson, James L., and Gregory A. Caldeira. 2003. Defenders of Democracy? Legitimacy, Popular Acceptance, and the South African Constitutional Court. *The Journal of Politics* 65 (1): 1–30. https://doi.org/10.1111/1468-2508.t01-1-00001.

Gibson, James, Gregory Caldeira, and Vanessa Baird. 1998. On the Legitimacy of National High Courts. *The American Political Science Review* 92 (June): 343. https://doi.org/10.2307/2585668.

Gutiérrez, Martha. 2022. “La Corte Constitucional frente a la Paz: control al acuerdo de paz de Colombia y su implementación.” *Reflexión Política* 24 (50): 50. https://doi.org/10.29375/01240781.4535.

Hamber, Brandon. 2002. Rights and Reasons: Challenges for Truth Recovery in South Africa and Northern Ireland. *Fordham Int'l LJ* 26: 1074.

International Criminal Court. 2021. “ICC Prosecutor, Mr Karim A. A. Khan QC, Concludes the Preliminary Examination of the Situation in Colombia with a Cooperation Agreement with the Government Charting the next Stage in Support of Domestic Efforts to Advance Transitional Justice." October 28. https://www.icc-cpi.int/news/icc-prosecutor-mr-karim-khan-qc-concludes-preliminary-examination-situation-colombia.

Invamer. 2024. "Encuesta Invamer Febrero 2024." February. https://caracoltv.brightspotcdn.com/2c/ae/5173738245abb2e043034a0c173a/encuesta-invamer-poll-febrero-2024.pdf.

JEP Press Office. 2019a. "La Sección de Revisión de la JEP aplica la garantía de no extradición a Seuxis Paucias Hernández." May 15. https://www.jep.gov.co:443/Sala-de-Prensa/Paginas/LA-SECCI%C3%93N-DE-REVISI%C3%93N-DE-LA-JEP-APLICA-LA-GARANT%C3%8DA-DE-NO-EXTRADICI%C3%93N-A-SEUXIS-PAUCIAS-HERN%C3%81NDEZ-SOLARTE.aspx.

JEP Press Office. 2019b. "Víctimas podrán participar en versiones de la Sala de Reconocimiento de la JEP." June 6. https://www.jep.gov.co:443/Sala-de-Prensa/Paginas/V%C3%ADctimas-podr%C3%A1n-participar-en-versiones-de-la-Sala-de-Reconocimiento-de-la-JEP.aspx.

JEP Press Office. 2020. "Tres historias para comprender los TOAR en la JEP." October 19. https://www.jep.gov.co:443/Sala-de-Prensa/Paginas/Tres-historias-para-comprender-los-TOAR-en-la-JEP.aspx.

JEP Press Office. 2023a. "JEP pide a Fiscalía que investigue conductas de antiguos servidores del ente acusador." March 6. https://www.jep.gov.co:443/Sala-de-Prensa/Paginas/jep-pide-a-fiscal%C3%ADa-que-investigue-conductas-de-antiguos-servidores-del-ente-acusador.aspx.

JEP Press Office. 2023b. "La JEP y la Fiscalía de la Corte Penal Internacional profundizan cooperación." June 6. https://www.jep.gov.co:443/Sala-de-Prensa/Paginas/la-jep-y-la-fiscalia-de-la-corte-penal-internacional-profundizan-cooperacion.aspx.

JEP Press Office. 2024. "JEP fortalece su mandato con Acuerdo de Complementariedad firmado entre el Gobierno y la Fiscalía de la Corte Penal Internacional." April 27. https://www.jep.gov.co:443/Sala-de-Prensa/Paginas/-jep-fortalece-su-mandato-con-acuerdo-de-complementariedad-firmado-entre-el-gobierno-y-la-fiscalia-de-la-corte-penal-intern.aspx.

Justice for Colombia [@JFColombia]. 2021. "During today's national strike protesters remember the 6,402 people killed by the Colombian Army in the 2000s. The Army offered false jobs to young people in poor neighbourhoods before murdering them and dressing them as guerrillas to increase their combat figures. #ParoNacional https://t.co/jRselQAWkr." Tweet. Twitter, April 28. https://twitter.com/JFColombia/status/1387481893139099651.

La Silla Vacía. 2024. "Colombia lanzará política de cooperación con la Corte Penal Internacional." La Silla Vacía, April 25. http://www.lasillavacia.com/en-vivo/colombia-lanzara-politica-de-cooperacion-con-la-corte-penal-internacional/.

Mauricio Albarracín Caballero [@malbarracin]. 2021. "#DiarioDeLaProtesta COEl número 6402 se ha convertido en un símbolo de las protestas en Colombia. Este número señala las ejecuciones extrajudiciales que @JEP_Colombia está investigando. Este número se puede ver en muchas partes de la ciudad pero ayer fue instalado en los Héroes https://t.co/7S8mhVqD0b." Tweet. Twitter, May 13. https://twitter.com/malbarracin/status/1392788404547510276.

Ospina-Pedraza, Ana María, Farid Samir Benavides-Vanegas, and Julián Darío Bonilla-Montenegro. 2023. "Keys to Interpreting the International Cooperation of the EU for the Special Jurisdiction for Peace." In *European Union Support for Colombia's Peace Process*, edited by Karlos Pérez De Armiño. Rethinking Peace and Conflict Studies. Springer Nature Switzerland. https://doi.org/10.1007/978-3-031-24797-2_10.

Paola Molano Ayala [@pmolanoayala]. 2024a. "La carta de @ComunesCoL al Presidente sobre la @JEP_Colombia, revela varias cosas preocupantes y urgentes de lado y lado 🧵." Tweet. Twitter, February 7. https://twitter.com/pmolanoayala/status/1755319474075345205.

Paola Molano Ayala [@pmolanoayala]. 2024b. "La decisión de la @JEP_Colombia de nombrar 36 magistrados auxiliares parece escandalosa, teniendo en cuenta que, con arandelas, son salarios de 37 millones de pesos. Además de esto, la decisión da lugar a, al menos, dos discusiones 🧵." Tweet. Twitter, February 5. https://twitter.com/pmolanoayala/status/1754328356038857146.

Partido COMUNES [@ComunesCoL]. 2024. "¿Por qué hablamos de 'descarrilamiento' de la #JEP? A 7 años de la firma del Acuerdo de paz, este es el avance de la jurisdicción ⬇️ 🧵https://t.co/zFIdgoD6C4." Tweet. Twitter, April 18. https://twitter.com/ComunesCoL/status/1780984818773188673.

Rebecca Brubaker. 2020. "The UN Security Council and Transitional Justice: Colombia." *United Nations University - Centre for Policy Research*, August. https://i.unu.edu/media/cpr.unu.edu/attachment/4844/UNU_TJ_Colombia.pdf.

Rodrigo Londoño. 2024. "Intervención en el Acto de comunicación de los decretos de amnistía de iure a firmantes del Acuerdo de Paz." X (formerly Twitter), February 21. https://twitter.com/TimoComunes.

Rodríguez-Raga, Juan Carlos. 2023. "El Barómetro de Las Américas Toma El Pulso de La Democracia En Colombia." In *Pulso de La Democracia En Colombia: 2023*. Barómetro de Las Américas. https://www.vanderbilt.edu/lapop/colombia/ABCOL2023-Pulso-de-la-democracia-final-20240403.pdf.

Semana. 2018. "El avispero que alborotó la JEP con el caso Santrich." Semana.com Últimas Noticias de Colombia y el Mundo, May 17. https://www.semana.com/caso-santrich-la-jep-levanto-un-avispero-con-suspension-de-extradicion/567484/.

Semana. 2019a. "La vigilia en París por la JEP." Semana.com Últimas Noticias de Colombia y el Mundo, March 9. https://www.semana.com/la-protesta-en-paris-por-la-posible-objecion-a-la-jep/604961/.
Semana. 2019b. "#YoDefiendoLaJEP: El mensaje que envían 30 líderes colombianos a Duque." Semana.com Últimas Noticias de Colombia y el Mundo, February 16. https://www.semana.com/yodefiendolajep-el-mensaje-que-envian-30-lideres-colombianos-a-duque/601741/.
Semana. 2020a. "Cero y van tres: un nuevo intento por modificar la JEP." Semana.com Últimas Noticias de Colombia y el Mundo, June 1. https://www.semana.com/cero-y-van-tres-un-nuevo-intento-por-modificar-la-jep/675534/.
Semana. 2020b. "JEP recibe millonario guiño de Europa." Semana.com Últimas Noticias de Colombia y el Mundo, July 28. https://www.semana.com/jep-recibe-millonario-guino-de-europa/689713/.
Semana. 2021. "'Quizás, quizás' y otros sarcasmos y cinismos de Santrich." Semana.com Últimas Noticias de Colombia y el Mundo, May 18. https://www.semana.com/nacion/articulo/quizas-quizas-y-otros-sarcasmos-y-cinismos-de-santrich/202118/.
Semana. 2023a. "Gobernadora del Valle cumplirá arresto desde este viernes y lanza duro dardo a la JEP: 'Criminales son nombrados gestores de paz.'" Semana.com Últimas Noticias de Colombia y el Mundo, December 28. https://www.semana.com/nacion/cali/articulo/gobernadora-del-valle-cumplira-arresto-desde-este-viernes-y-lanza-duro-dardo-a-la-jep-criminales-son-nombrados-gestores-de-paz/202350/.
Semana. 2023b. "Por insultar a la víctimas y llamar 'guerrilleros' a los magistrados, la JEP pide investigar penal y disciplinariamente al alcalde de Aguachica (Cesar)." Semana.com Últimas Noticias de Colombia y el Mundo, May 31. https://www.semana.com/nacion/articulo/por-insultar-a-la-victimas-y-llamar-guerrilleros-a-los-magistrados-la-jep-pide-investigar-penal-y-disciplinariamente-al-alcalde-de-aguachica-cesar/202329/.
Semana. 2024a. "Atención | JEP le responde al Secretariado de las Farc. De renunciar a comparecer perderán todos los beneficios y enfrentarán la justicia ordinaria." Semana.com Últimas Noticias de Colombia y el Mundo, February 7. https://www.semana.com/nacion/articulo/atencion-jep-le-responde-al-secretariado-de-las-farc-de-renunciar-a-comparecer-perderan-todos-los-beneficios-y-enfrentaran-la-justicia-ordinaria/202418/.

Semana. 2024b. "'Completa falsedad': magistrado Roberto Vidal les responde a excomandantes de las Farc y recuerda los 60 años de cárcel que purgarán si la JEP no les gusta." Semana.com Últimas Noticias de Colombia y el Mundo, February 27. https://www.semana.com/semana-tv/vicky-en-semana/articulo/completa-falsedad-magistrado-roberto-vidal-les-responde-a-excomandantes-de-las-farc-y-recuerda-los-60-anos-de-carcel-que-purgaran-si-la-jep-no-les-gusta/202429/.

Shany, Yuval. 2014. Assessing the Effectiveness of International Courts. *Oxford University Press*. https://doi.org/10.1093/acprof:oso/9780199643295.001.0001.

Theodor Meron. 2003. "ICTY Oral History - Theodor Meron." Interview by ICTY Oral History Collection. October 20. https://ictyoralhistory.sensecentar.org/theodor-meron-interview.

UN Verification Mission and JEP. 2022. "La JEP y la Misión de la ONU firman protocolo que activa el Mecanismo de Monitoreo y Verificación de las Sanciones Propias." August 16. https://www.jep.gov.co:443/Sala-de-Prensa/Paginas/La-JEP-y-la-Misi%C3%B3n-de-la-ONU-firman-protocolo-que-activa-el-Mecanismo-de-Monitoreo-y-Verificaci%C3%B3n-de-las-Sanciones-Propias-.aspx.

Uprimny, Yepes, Rodrigo, Maria Paula Saffón Sanin, Catalina Botero Marino, and Esteban Restrepo Saldarriaga. 2006. *¿Justicia Transicional Sin Transición? Verdad, Justicia y Reparación Para Colombia*. Dejusticia. https://www.dejusticia.org/wp-content/uploads/2017/04/fi_name_recurso_201.pdf.

Van Hoeven, Juliana. 2016. *Counter-Terrorism Measures and International Humanitarian Law: A Case Study of the "Troubles" in Northern Ireland*.

Yesid Reyes. 2024. "Los reclamos de las extintas FARC-EP a la JEP." Text. ELESPECTADOR.COM, February 13. https://www.elespectador.com/opinion/columnistas/yesid-reyes-alvarado/los-reclamos-de-las-extintas-farc-ep-a-la-jep/.

CHAPTER 6

Conclusions

Abstract The conclusion chapter summarises the book's arguments. It stresses the importance of addressing the pressing issues of the delays in handing down definitive rulings, balancing the victims' participation with the need for definitive results, and the need for better explaining and communicating the JEP's operation to the Colombian society. Finally, it posits some lessons for peace-building processes in other areas of the world. Institutional efforts to educate society and especially involved actors on restorative justice are essential to guarantee legitimacy and support from national and international organisations is important to ensure the system's operation, notably during times where it is heavily criticised. Similarly, having an effective administrative design is essential to increase efficiency and effectiveness in the operation so that ruling are not delayed; and conducting hearings and the framing of rulings also play an important role when it comes to strengthening legitimacy.

Keywords Transitional justice challenges · Peace-building processes · National support · International support · Procedural delays

In this book, I addressed the question of the sociological legitimacy of the JEP. This issue is important because the literature on the legitimacy

N. Zuluaga Afanador, *The Sociological Legitimacy of the Special Jurisdiction for Peace of Colombia*, St Antony's Series,
https://doi.org/10.1007/978-3-032-21912-1_6

of transitional justice legal systems is scarce and maintaining legitimacy is essential to accomplish the JEP's goals. First, I argued in favour of studying sociological legitimacy, beyond a normative approach, since the critiques against the JEP are usually moral and concern emotions, and the JEP's legal legitimacy is not contested. Then, I endeavoured to provide a method to study sociological legitimacy as a contribution to the academic literature and the JEP itself. A framework serves to highlight the flaws in operation, successes and failures. It condenses what might be perceived in day-to-day operations.

Using a range of sources, I sought to probe whether the factors of legitimacy that academic literature for high courts posited were useful to understand the JEP's sociological legitimacy. I selected the most recurrent factors of legitimacy in the existing literature and, given that the academic literature had scarcely explained ways to operationalise them, I proposed some signs of erosion or strengthening of such factors and a scale to gauge them. Certainly, there are limitations on this research project: the time and budget available were insufficient to carry out surveys, which might produce more generalisable assumptions. Yet, with the available sources, I conveyed an idea of the JEP's sociological legitimacy, being as rigorous as possible with the information in hand.

This is the main reason for the focus on historical background, to help the reader understand the issues that may affect the sociological legitimacy of the JEP today. In the final section before the conclusion, I test the theoretical framework against the development of a transitional justice jurisdiction that has been operating for more than seven years, with around 1,000–1,300 employees, and that pursues ambitious goals. This operation has unfolded in a complex political context, where the internal armed conflict has not stopped and the vestiges of war are still latent. In general, the JEP's sociological legitimacy has increased over time, as I described in the section on diffuse support, especially regarding the frustrated attempts to modify its structure. Thanks to medium levels of diffuse support, obedience, and salience and, to a lesser extent specific support, the JEP's sociological legitimacy is at a medium level that could begin dropping lower This measure explains the JEP's capacity to make contentious decisions, maintain its structure, increase its personnel, as well as its ability to hand down decisions that are enforced, but it also explains the increasing criticisim to its effectiveness.

Three main issues are significantly eroding the JEP's sociological legitimacy: (1) the lack of definitive rulings on all levels—both for "most responsible" *comparecientes* and for non-"most responsible" *comparecientes*. If it does not hand down a significant number of definitive decisions, the JEP will not meet the expectations of justice from the victims and society, and of legal certainty from the *comparecientes*. It might be perceived as an ineffective court. (2) The victims' participation has been criticised. This is precisely a trade-off between the participation of victims and the principle of strict temporality—the more victims participate, the slower the process might be, and vice versa. Nonetheless, the JEP should look for ways of addressing the victims' concerns while speeding up processes. (3) The JEP's functioning is still unknown to most Colombians. This prevents them from increasing their trust in the JEP and accepting the JEP's restorative justice paradigm.

The JEP's case can also underpin peace building in other areas of the world that are experiencing armed conflicts. Policymakers and stakeholders of future and existing transitional justice courts could learn from the JEP's case that pedagogy is essential to ensure trust from society, especially for a new court that attempts to implement restorative justice and change the punitive paradigm. If people understand how the Court works, they will be more likely to support and defend it. Moreover, support from national and international institutions is essential. The endorsement of high courts, Congress, the ICC and UN agencies to a transitional justice court makes changes in its structure less likely to happen. Victims' participation is also a necessary condition to ensure their support. This, along with the support of national and international institutions, heavily strengthens the legitimacy of a transitional justice tribunal.

Having an effective administrative design might be equally important. It is essential to achieve effectiveness, by using efficiently limited resources in promptly handing down definitive rulings and preventing delays that hamper loyalty and trust. The framing of the rulings also plays an important role: word choice, argumentation, and the legal sources used are fields where transitional justice courts defend their independence and convince audiences of their authority. Hearings are opportunities where the court educates on its operation, justifies its existence, argues its benefits, showcases its processes and, foremost, reinforces its symbols. The JEP's case may show that there is nothing more legitimising than getting the work done (and communicating it).

Effectively advancing the transition to peace in Colombia is not an easy task. Past decades of violence still affect the present situation. Present armed conflicts perpetuate violence, while transitional justice institutions try to contribute to healing the wounds that the armed conflict between the Government and the FARC-EP inflicted. This book helps to understand how the JEP is perceived by Colombian society and how various factors can contribute to its legitimacy. In doing so, it will hopefully contribute to building peace in Colombia and support other peace processes around the world.

CHAPTER 7

Epilogue: The First Two Proper Sanctions and Their Impact on Legitimacy

Abstract After this book was written, the Section of Acknowledgement of Responsibility and Truth issued the first two sentences imposing proper sanctions for kidnapping cases against the former top commanders of the FARC-EP and for extrajudicial killings committed by the "La Popa" Battalion in the Caribbean Coast. Given the importance of the rulings, this section describes their content and offers a preliminary evaluation of their impact on the JEP's sociological legitimacy. The issuing of these two sentences potentially increased the importance of the obedience to the rulings as a factor to legitimacy, while specific support to them seems low and diffuse support is decreasing. In addition, the JEP faces several obstacles to make the perpetrators and the State as a whole comply with the proper sanctions. The chapter concludes with some remarks on the impact of these rulings in the JEP's operations and future, both as an international potential model of a transitional justice tribunal and as an example of Colombia's efforts to build a long-standing stable peace.

Keywords Restorative justice · Retributive justice · Proper sanctions · Inter-institutional cooperation · Compliance with rulings · Restriction of liberties · Political rights · Mistrust · FARC-EP · Armed Forces

N. Zuluaga Afanador, *The Sociological Legitimacy of the Special Jurisdiction for Peace of Colombia*, St Antony's Series,
https://doi.org/10.1007/978-3-032-21912-1_7

7.1 Epilogue: The First Two Proper Sanctions and Their Impact on Legitimacy

In September 2025, the SeRVR finally handed down the first two proper sanction sentences in the macro-cases 1 and 3. Following the JEP's established practice of delivering important rulings to both FARC-EP and Armed Forces members within a short period of time, on September 16, 2025, the Section imposed proper sanctions to the seven surviving former members of the FARC-EP Secretariat in the macro-case 1. Two days later, the same Section announced its first sentence against twelve former members of the "La Popa" Battalion on the Caribbean Coast, within a sub-case of the macro-case 3.

The rulings were published months after this book was written. However, due to their importance, this chapter will describe their content and offer a preliminarily evaluation of their implications for the JEP's sociological legitimacy.

7.2 The Sentence Against the Surviving Members of the FARC-EP Secretariat

On September 16, 2025, at the JEP headquarters in Bogotá, Camilo Suárez Aldana, former judge of the military jurisdiction for fourteen years and Judge Rapporteur in the macro-case 1, announced at a press conference that the SeRVR had issued a sentence against the seven surviving members of the FARC-EP Secretariat, including the organisation's top commander, Rodrigo Londoño Echeverri (JEP Press Office 2025). After acknowledging responsibility for the crimes, the Section determined that these individuals were perpetrators of serious international crimes (Section of Acknowledgement of Responsibility and Truth 2025a).

The Tribunal found they had committed war crimes of hostage-taking and homicide, as well as the crimes against humanity of severe deprivation of physical liberty, enforced disappearance and murder. The convicted individuals were held responsible for the kidnapping of more than 21,000 people between 1993 and 2012, as well as for multiple crimes committed in connection with these acts.

Similarly, under the doctrine of command responsibility, the FARC-EP former top commanders were found responsible for the war crimes of torture, sexual violence and forced displacement, as well as for the crimes against humanity of torture and enslavement, among others.

Although the FARC-EP had engaged in kidnapping since its early years, the investigation prioritised the period between 1993 and 2012 and established that these atrocities were part of a criminal policy based on three nationwide patterns (Section of Acknowledgement of Responsibility and Truth 2025a, 14–25). First, since 1993, the FARC-EP adopted an internal policy to use these crimes to fund the organisation. Guerrilla members were expected to identify wealthy individuals for kidnapping and to use ransom payments to collect funds. Yet, in practice, many regional commanders authorised the abduction of individuals whose wealth was not clearly identified, due to the pressure to meet a quota to finance the guerrilla's national strategic plan.

The second pattern consisted of the deprivation of liberty of both Armed Forces officers and civilians for the purpose of exchanging them for imprisoned guerrillas. This policy was initially adopted in 1997 and targeted members of the Security Forces, particularly during guerrilla takeovers of Army bases and police stations. When this strategy did not have the expected results, the top FARC-EP commanders extended this policy in 2001 to civilians perceived as "politicians", including governmental authorities and public figures. For instance, following this directive, in 2002, the FARC-EP Western Joint Command kidnapped 12 deputies of the Departmental Assembly of Valle del Cauca in Cali. Eleven were murdered as the Army was trying to rescue them; only Sigifredo López survived and was released in 2009. Despite the FARC-EP's intentions, these crimes were not successful in forcing a prisoners' exchange with the Government (Section of Acknowledgement of Responsibility and Truth 2025a, 20).

As for the third pattern, mainly in the areas where the FARC-EP were created or the State was weak or non-existent, the guerrilla organisation exercised control over social life by mediating local disputes, regulating the use of common goods like water and managing landownership. Not all community members supported these actions, and the guerrilla resorted to abducting local politicians, wealthy residents and people accused of sympathising and helping paramilitary groups or rival guerrillas to reinforce its territorial control.

The punishment for the most responsible of these macro-criminal patterns was the most severe punishment the Section could impose. All seven living members of the FARC-EP Secretariat were sentenced to eight years of proper sanctions. As a result, they are required to carry out TOAR projects under the following four general lines of action, while their liberty is restricted. The project areas are: (1) the search for persons deemed missing; (2) a comprehensive action programme against anti-personnel mines; (3) environment, nature and territory; and (4) memory and symbolic reparation.

These proposals resulted from a restorative and dialogical process between perpetrators and victims before both the SRVR and SeRVR. Both instances organised meetings in which, with the support of their attorneys, the *comparecientes* presented their proposals while the victims expressed their views, described their expectations and suggested TOAR projects (Section of Acknowledgement of Responsibility and Truth 2025a, 311–16).

In particular, the Section developed a participative strategy to foster restorative spaces for dialogue and to ensure that victims could effectively contribute to the design of the projects. To this end, it organised several meetings as a part of a participatory restorative process. These included hearings during which victims commented on the projects presented before the SRVR, throughout 2023 and in the first semester of 2024; coordination meetings, in November 2024 and throughout 2025, involving public institutions and the *comparecientes'* attorneys to align coordination around the four lines of projects; and additional hearings and dialogue spaces, in December 2024 and June 2025, that enabled victims to comment on the final project designs.

As for the lines of projects, the first, "Memory and symbolic reparation", consists of activities aimed at dignifying the victims' memory. *Comparecientes* will transcribe victims' testimonies, construct memorial tiles honouring the victims' lives and participate in radio and audiovisual documentaries, among other TOAR initiatives related to the symbolic reparation and collective memory.

Concerning the "Search for people deemed missing", the convicted individuals must compile a report of available information held by the FARC-EP members regarding reported missing persons. They are also required to share this information with the UBPD, contributing to the provision of coordinates indicating the possible location of victims' remains. Moreover, they are expected to assist in identifying bodies that remain unidentified in cemeteries and other locations. A TOAR at the cemetery of Palmira, a town in Southwestern Colombia, has been identified as the initial intervention ordered by this sentence.

Regarding "Environment, nature, and territory", the *comparecientes* are required to plant native species affected by the internal armed conflict and contribute to subsistence crops of local peasants.

Finally, in relation to action against anti-personnel mines, they must provide new information on affected territories, techniques and tactics employed, and draft cartographic materials. They must also support the preparation of demining procedures and carry out outreach activities in connection with these projects.

7.2.1 Controversial Elements: Restriction of Liberty and Political Rights

The retributive component of the sentence was less well defined, causing several negative reactions across different audiences. The SeRVR did not clearly establish the perimeter within which the *comparecientes* could move, their place of residence or the specific details of the surveillance methods and devices to be employed.

Instead, the Section laid down general guidelines for monitoring compliance with the sanctions. It retained the authority to approve any permission to leave the designated area for fulfilling the proper sanction and to engage in activities outside the prescribed working hours (2025a, 526). Without much detail, it ordered that those convicted carry a non-invasive electronic device, like a Personal Digital Assistant, that would trigger an alert if the defendant transgressed the established perimeter (2025a, 530–32).

To verify and monitor the fulfilment of the restrictions of liberty, the Section created a three-level monitoring system comprising: the UN Verification Mission, as the international component; the Executive Secretariat through its technical departments operating in an administrative monitoring support role; and the SeRVR, as the judicial verification body (2025a, 536–43).

As an international authority, the UN Verification Mission was expected to verify with objectivity, transparency and rigour that the TOAR projects were properly implemented, as well as to provide technical assistance and to submit reports to the Security Council. Nonetheless, the Security Council recently decided that the UN Verification Mission would not be assigned the function of monitoring proper sanctions. This situation and its impact on the JEP's sociological legitimacy will be better explained below.

The JEP's Executive Secretariat carries out the daily monitoring tasks. It collects the information about the projects' execution, directly oversees their progress and the orders' compliance, articulates the cooperation with other State Agencies and reports this information to the Section.

Using the UN Verification Mission and the Executive Secretariat information, the Section verifies the compliance with the judicial terms and certifies whether the *comparecientes* fulfilled the sanctions. When they have presumably breached the sanctions' terms, it investigates these events and, if necessary, delivers the correspondent sanctions.

In terms of political participation, the Section found reasonable that, in order to build peace and strengthen democracy, the proper sanctions would not curtail the use of political rights, as one of the FARC's motivations to sign the Peace Agreement was participating in the political system (2025a, 240). Yet, the judicial authority pointed out two caveats: whenever the execution of political functions becomes impossible to reconcile with the implementation of proper sanctions, the latter should prevail. Furthermore, political rights cannot be used to deliver negationist and victimising discourses.

7.3 The Sentence Against the Armed Forces Agents of "La Popa" Battalion

On September 18, 2025, led by the Judge Rapporteur Ana Manuela Ochoa, descendant from the Kankuamo Indigenous People, the SeRVR found that 12 former Members of the "La Popa" Battalion of the Army were responsible for the assassination of at least 135 people who were falsely presented between January 2002 and July 2005 as guerrilla casualties in the Caribbean Region, in the North of Colombia (Section of Acknowledgement of Responsibility and Truth 2025b). The victims were women, children, peasants, indigenous people and afrodescendants, many of them in situations of vulnerability. They were profiled, deceived, detained and executed by State agents who were supposed to protect them. Some of these crimes also involved torture and enforced disappearance, and they all constituted crimes against humanity, which were committed following two patterns.

In the first pattern, atrocities were carried out with the complicity of paramilitary groups from the North Bloc of the AUC. Paramilitary members or civilian accomplices identified the victims as FARC collaborators, who were later killed by paramilitary groups or Armed Forces agents (Section of Acknowledgement of Responsibility and Truth 2025b, 34–37).

The second pattern consisted of crimes against people in vulnerable situations who were either arbitrarily detained or deceived by members of "La Popa" Battalion with false promises of employment, business opportunities or money. Victims worked in informal economic activities, such recycling materials or street vending; others were simply sleeping on the street. Many were transported from other regions of Colombia, which made them more difficult to identify (Section of Acknowledgement of Responsibility and Truth 2025b, 37–39).

The twelve *comparecientes* were sentenced to proper sanctions ranging from five to nine years of executing TOAR projects and restriction of liberties, according to their level of responsibility. Before handing down the ruling, between August 2023 and June 2025, the SeRVR held around 15 meetings and hearings in which the victims and the *comparecientes* dialogued to agree on the restorative projects, while public institutions coordinated to put the TOAR initiatives into place. The Section actively tried to include José Prudencio Padilla and Kusuto MaGende Afro-Colombian Communitarian Councils, holding several of these events in their territories, as well as the Wiwa and Kankuamo Indigenous Peoples.

Following this participatory process, the SeRVR established six projects through which defendants could comply with the proper sanctions. Unlike in the case against the FARC-EP, this ruling is more precise in regulating the activities to be undertaken in every project, the sources of funding, the specific harms each initiative expects to repair and the preliminary execution timelines for implementation (Section of Acknowledgement of Responsibility and Truth 2025b, 457–80).

First, the Integral Plan of Historical Memory for the Caribbean Coast includes the construction of memory parks across the region, memorial infrastructure at La Popa Battalion and a memory mausoleum of 700 ossuaries in Valledupar—a medium-size city within the case's geographical scope. Furthermore, this initiative aims to reframe the narrative about *falsos positivos* through communication campaigns and symbolic reparation acts (Section of Acknowledgement of Responsibility and Truth 2025b, 462).

Second, the Harmonization Centre for the Good Living of the Families of the Kankuamo People involves improving cultural and transportation infrastructure, and implementing actions to restore the tropical dry forest as a means of taking care of the Mother Earth and the Kankuamo's sacred sites (Section of Acknowledgement of Responsibility and Truth 2025b, 458).

Third, the Comprehensive Cultural and Historic Memory Centre in the Wiwa People's territory is expected to become a cultural and spiritual venue for promoting the ancestral memory of the community. Fourth, the Cultural House in the Afro-descendent José Prudencio Pradilla Communitarian Council serves a similar purpose in that community.

Fifth, perpetrators are required to construct Multipurpose Houses for victims in Valledupar. These spaces are intended to provide young people with guidance on educational and employment opportunities, as well as mental health and psychosocial attention.

Sixth, in the "Sowers of Love and Peace" project, *comparecientes* will contribute to strengthening the capacities of victims from the Kusuto MaGende Communitarian Council to develop productive projects in fishing, agriculture and ecotourism.

7.3.1 Restriction of Liberty and Political Rights

With respect to restrictions on liberty, the ruling in the macro-case 3 is more specific than the sentence in the macro-case 1 (Section of Acknowledgement of Responsibility and Truth 2025b, 431–37). It defines the concrete activities the defendants would start undertaking—works at the ossuaries of the Ecce Homo Cemetery in Valledupar. It further orders that they must travel to the TOAR locations by their own means; sets the working hours from Monday to Friday (8 a.m. to 12 p.m., and from 2 p.m. to 5 p.m.); and provides that the *comparecientes* will live in public housing in Valledupar, have access to health insurance and receive living expenses and security protection from the Ministry of Defence.

Moreover, the convicted individuals may not change place of residence or leave the country without permission from the Section; they must report weekly to the JEP's Executive Secretariat, primarily in person; and they must use an electronic monitoring device. At the same time, they may have access to social media, provided that they do not publish content that revictimises the victims or impacts their security.

As for political rights, the Section is required to assess how the *comparecientes*' participation in politics is compatible with the proper sanctions and, in particular, with the TOAR.

Lastly, the mechanisms for monitoring the fulfilment of the sanctions are the same as those established in case of the FARC-EP leadership.

7.4 How Do These Rulings Impact the JEP's Legitimacy?

This section describes how the sentences in the macro-cases 1 and 3 have impacted the JEP's legitimacy in the short period since they have been handed down. This assessment is preliminary, and further research should study how the implementation of the proper sanctions shapes the JEP's legitimacy over time.

7.4.1 The Specific Support for the Rulings Is Low, Especially for the Macro-case 1 Sentence

Based on the sources analysed—opinion columns, news coverage and television programmes—there seems to be limited support for these rulings. Following the signs of legitimacy strengthening or eroding explained in Table 3.2 of Sect. 3.4, I did not identify generalised signs of satisfaction towards the decisions. The significant delay in issuing these decisions impacted different audiences' perceptions on their contribution on peace, and the balance in addressing the investigations against the FARC-EP and the Armed Forces was contested.

On the contrary, I could observe strong consistent critiques of the decisions and the JEP itself, as well as salient cases of opposition and framing issues, particularly in the macro-case 1 sentence. It is possible that certain audiences are more receptive to the sentence in the "Caribbean Coast" sub-case of the macro-case 3. One factor that might work in its favour is that the terms of the proper sanction are clearer—the place of residence and the specifics of the projects are more defined, it has a stronger territorial grounding, and the impact of projects on the communities is more tangible. In addition, the sentence appears to be the result of a process that may have provided more truth than the macro-case 1 sentence, given that the victims could engage directly with perpetrators more directly connected to the crimes.

These nuances are more visible in the reactions among victims across the different cases. Most victims of the FARC-EP expressed their dissatisfaction. Many pointed out that, in their opinion, the FARC-EP top commanders had not provided all the truth available to them and the sentence did not adequately restore the victims' rights.

For example, Sigifredo López said that the FARC-EP members did not confess who their accomplices to break into the Departmental Assembly were. This information was important to him, since López was put in jail for being falsely accused of supporting the guerrilla (Torres Lasso 2025). Another victim, Jhon Contreras, stated that former FARC-EP members have never said why they kidnapped his mother or where she is (Torres Lasso 2025). The prominent Ingrid Betancourt, a former Presidential Candidate kidnapped in February 2002 for more than six years, claimed that she was going to appeal the decision and resort to international instances, if necessary. In her own words, "what happened today is a mockery of all the people who were kidnapped. When you look at the sentence and the list of sanctions they apply to them, it is outrageous"[1] (Gómez 2025).

Clara Rojas, Betancourt's former running mate, who was also kidnapped alongside her, has publicly questioned the proportionality of the sentence imposed on the FARC-EP Secretariat. In a post on her X account, she expressed her dissatisfaction, summarising many of the critiques raised by victims:

> This sentence is not proportional to the immensity of the harm caused to 21,800 victims. There is not total truth either, which under the law would have allowed tougher sanctions. Their political rights are preserved, there is not a direct form of reparation, neither economic nor moral. A sense of impunity remains. So much time has passed, so much noise, so much instrumentalization of the victims, zero reparation.[2] (Clara Rojas [@CLARAROJASG] 2025)

This tweet represents a salient dissatisfaction with the macro-case 1 judicial process. Rojas participated before the SRVR in the early stages of the JEP, but her current opinions convey a feeling that the first JEP sentence was unfair and disproportionate. In her view, sanctions could have been more severe, the *comparecientes* did not provide all the truth

[1] Quote in Spanish: "Lo ocurrido hoy es una burla para todas las personas que estuvimos secuestradas. Cuando uno mira la sentencia y ve el listado de penas que les aplican, es indignante".

[2] Quote in Spanish: "Esta sentencia no tiene proporcionalidad con la inmensidad del daño causado a 21.800 víctimas. Tampoco hay verdad total, lo cual permitía sanciones más altas, como lo prevee la ley. Les mantienen derechos politicos, tampoco hay ningún tipo de reparación directa, ni económica ni moral. Queda la impunidad en el aire. Mucho tiempo transcurrido, mucho ruido, mucha instrumentalización de las víctimas, cero reparación".

they knew, and victims remained without reparation, while perpetrators may continue to exercise their political rights.

Similarly, Cesar Augusto Lasso, a former Army colonel who was held captive by the FARC-EP for 14 years, and Juan Camilo San Clemente, attorney of the families of the 11 kidnapped Deputies of Valle del Cauca, have claimed that the sentences are a sign of impunity (Osorio 2025; León 2025). Lasso added that, as a captive, he was unable to see his children grow up, was frequently chained to another companion, and many times had to eat once a day. As a result, he was expecting a harsher and more meaningful expression of justice.

Other victims have argued that the FARC-EP's top commanders have not fulfilled their demands of truth. Olga González is one of them. A few months ago, she and her family recovered her father's body, more than 13 years after he was kidnapped. Despite this restorative event, she maintains that they are still hoping for the *comparecientes* to tell the truth, and solve questions like: "What happened after they took their father from the place he was in? What happened since he was kidnapped until the day he died?". In her words, "we want that truth, we want to know what happened, we want to know the why, and that truth has not arrived"[3] (Mesa Loaiza 2025).

In a sentence that sanctions the top commanders of the armed organisation, that truth is difficult to emerge. Defendants are not necessarily directly related to the crimes done to the victims, and they are held responsible not for specific crimes, but for executing broader patterns of victimisation.

However, some journalists and victims have more favourable opinions of the sentences, particularly among those associated with the macro-case 3 (Torres Lasso 2025). Néstor Oñate declared that those who should have protected his brother, Marquis, killed him, and he only had the chance of clearing his brother's name when the Army agents confessed he was not a guerrilla member.

Similarly, the *kankuamo* Oseas Arias recognised the restorative aspect of the process. He asserted that:

> As Kankuamo indigenous people, this was what we expected. We are in touch with some of the *comparecientes*, and this relationship has even

[3] Quote in Spanish: "Nosotros queremos esa verdad, queremos saber qué pasó, queremos saber el por qué y esa verdad no ha llegado".

allowed us to offer them our support, despite the mistakes and failures they committed. Some of us are going to participate with them. There are six reparation projects, and now we hope the funding will be available.[4]

In the days following the issuance of the sentences, journalists Juanita León and Héctor Riveros noted that these decisions undermined the narrative that perpetrators involved in *falsos positivos* were isolated exceptions. The rulings also transformed the FARC-EP members' discourse, from initially denying the possibility of compensating the victims, as illustrated by Santrich's statement that the group would "perhaps" collaborate in addressing the victims' rights, as discussed in Sect. 5.1.3.1, to publicly acknowledging that the kidnapping policy was a mistake and the top commanders were responsible for war crimes and crimes against humanity (La Silla Vacía 2025).

One common aspect in both cases is that victims expressed a feeling of impunity. This impression shows that the JEP could not convince many of them that proper sanctions, an especially restorative justice, were a satisfactory alternative to conventional punitive sanctions. Even though the Agreement defined that if *comparecientes* fully cooperated, they would not go to jail and victims could not claim compensation, many victims have prison and material compensation as a yardstick for justice. The beliefs and values around justice in some audiences did not change and sanctions were perceived as too lenient.

Among these mixed reactions, it seems that victims from the macro-case 3 are more satisfied with the rulings than those from the macro-case 1. Why?

First, as stated above, the macro-case 3 sanctions' terms are clearer. Unlike the macro-case 1 sentence, the macro-case 3 ruling established the *comparecientes'* place of residence, specified the sources of funding for every project and set out a clearer list of activities. The projects are more directly connected to the harm inflicted on the communities and respond to their specific needs. Furthermore, the fact that the Judge Rapporteur is a member of one of the Kakuamo indigenous people may

[4] Quote in Spanish: "Como indígenas kankuamo, esto era lo que esperábamos. Estamos en contacto con algunos de los comparecientes, e incluso esta relación nos ha permitido brindarles nuestro apoyo, a pesar de los errores y fracasos que cometieron. Algunos de nosotros vamos a participar con ellos. Existen seis proyectos de reparación, y ahora esperamos que los recursos estén disponibles".

have contributed not only to reinforce their sense of representativity, but also to perform more adequate framing mechanisms.

For example, as Gabriel Rojas pointed out, during the public reading of La Popa sentence, the document was introduced in a *mochila*, a hand-crafted traditional bag which in this context symbolised a shared sense of grief and memory and, in many Colombian Indigenous communities, represents a spiritual process of weaving and reproducing the world. Furthermore, the members of the Section read aloud a poem describing the painful consequences of extrajudicial killings on the victims' families, as well as the victims' names one by one, while conveying that the State accompanied their pain (Rojas 2025). By contrast, there is no report of similar framing mechanisms deployed during the macro-case 1 public reading of the sentence.

Moreover, although in both macro-cases the monitoring system for controlling the restriction of liberty is still vague, in the macro-case 1 there is not a clear definition of the defendants' place of residence. This is something the Human Rights Watch director for the Americas Division and former Colombian Government peace negotiator, Juanita Goebertus pointed out in her X account. She expressed concern that the Section had avoided defining the perimeter within which the defendants would be restrained (Juanita Goebertus [@JuanitaGoe] 2025). This problem of ambiguous framing forced the Judge Rapporteur Suárez to clarify a few days later that the Section would issue follow-up rulings specifying the conditions regulating restrictions on liberty conditions and the implementation of the restorative projects (María Jimena Duzán 2025).

There is another source of dissatisfaction that may connect the erosion of the specific support with a decline in diffuse support. This is the fact that many victims remain sceptical as to whether the sacrifices made in the name of justice were justified when there is not a perceived peace in return, as Colombia still faces armed confrontations with the only surviving guerrilla group, the ELN, and other organised armed groups primarily linked to illegal economies.

This concern reinforces the importance of the discussion described in Sect. 5.3 on the difficulties in implementing a transitional justice model without a clear transition. As Colonel Lasso expressed it: "There is no imprisonment, no compensation and no form of reparation whatsoever

[...] However, if this process with the JEP had brought peace, fine, one would endure the sacrifice"[5] (León 2025).

Others support the ruling while they remain sceptical. A kidnapping victim stressed that tension:

> The lack of justice is enormous, but it is the price we had to pay to end violence. We knew that the only way for them to demobilise, agree to the Peace Agreement, and reintegrate into the civilian life was for them not go to jail. That is the price we victims paid and we had to sacrifice ourselves so that the violence stopped at that moment. But today we look at our country and we ask ourselves the question: Is it worth stopping the violence when it is re-emerging again? If in my personal case I have to forget that to avoid deaths from 2016 onward, well, I have nothing to say, only to be strong and turn the page.[6] (Mesa Loaiza 2025)

The sentences are still perceived as unfair, as a price victims must pay on behalf of the whole society to reduce violence. However, when violence resurges, as it has in recent years, the terms of this trade-off seem less reasonable.

Further, as observed by Humberto de la Calle, former chief negotiator for the Government at the Peace Negotiations with the FARC-EP, the delays in handing down definitive rulings affected people's perspectives on the effectiveness of the JEP. In an opinion article, he argued that as the cruellest period of violence becomes more distant from the moment when the rulings were published, it is easier to say that the penalties are derisory (De la Calle Lombana 2025). Thus, time impacts the satisfaction of the different audiences towards decisions.

[5] Quote in Spanish: "No hay ni cárcel, ni indemnización, ni ningún tipo de reparación [...] Ahora —agrega—, si este proceso con la JEP hubiese traído paz, listo, uno aguanta el sacrificio".

[6] Quote in Spanish: "El vacío de justicia es grande, pero es el precio que teníamos que pagar para acabar con la violencia. Sabíamos que la única manera de que ellos se entregaran y accedieran al Acuerdo de Paz, a incorporarse a la vida civil, era no pagar cárcel. Ese es el precio que pagamos las víctimas y tuvimos que sacrificarnos con el fin de que se hubiese apagado la violencia en ese momento. Pero miramos hoy en día nuestro país y nos hacemos la pregunta ¿Vale la pena parar la violencia cuando está resurgiendo nuevamente? Si en mi caso personal tengo que olvidarme de eso para haber evitado las muertes del 2016 hacía acá, pues no tengo nada que decir, solo sacar fortaleza y pasar la página".

7.4.2 *Diffuse Support for the JEP*

The different reactions to the JEP's first sentences show that many audiences mistrust the JEP, and that those who had been sceptical since its inception became more entrenched in their beliefs, while the international community continues to support the JEP's operation. However, one of the most important allies, the United States Government, has expressed doubts about the JEP, which led the UN Verification Mission to stop monitoring the fulfilment of proper sanctions. This development may ultimately undermine effectiveness of the proper sanctions.

Following the publication of both sentences, those who have been opposed to the JEP since its inception intensified their critiques and some claimed that these rulings confirmed that their original objections were well founded. On his X account, Álvaro Uribe Vélez argued that the JEP was unnecessary. In his opinion, Armed Forces agents have confessed crimes they did not commit to ensure their liberty, something which he and his party had warned the Santos Government about (Álvaro Uribe Vélez [@AlvaroUribeVel] 2025).

After the JEP handed down the two sentences, Francisco Santos—an opponent of the 2016 Peace Agreement, Vice President during the Uribe Administration and cousin of former president Juan Manuel Santos—claimed that the JEP's opponents were right: the tribunal guaranteed impunity to the FARC-EP leaders (Santos 2025). He argued that the seven FARC-EP members sentenced would not fulfil their sanctions—they will not risk their lives demining territories, lacked information to locate missing persons and would, at most, plant trees for environmental restoration.

Furthermore, he asserted, the sanctions are not proportional to the crimes committed. By contrast, paramilitaries were imprisoned under the Justice and Peace process, while guerrilla leaders now serve as Congressmen. This disparity, he contended, demonstrates that FARC-EP war crimes do not have a punishment—planting trees suffices as accountability. In a few words, "today with this ruling, an impartial justice legitimises the use of violence by punishing it with symbols that will not even be fulfilled" (Santos 2025).[7]

[7] Quote in Spanish: "Hoy con este fallo, una justicia entregada legitima el uso de la violencia al castigarla con símbolos que ni siquiera se van a cumplir".

The international support for the JEP has somewhat changed after the Section sentences, although in general terms it is still strong and aims at preventing that political changes interfere with the JEP's operation. Once the rulings were issued, the UN High Commissioner for Human Rights, Volker Türk, stated that they were "a crucial milestone on the path to accountability" and "a fundamental step in the fight against impunity and in fulfilling the rights of victims to truth and justice" (Mishra 2025). Similarly, the UN Secretary-General António Guterres noted that the rulings represented a step forward, and underlined that the UN, including the UN Verification Mission, remained "firmly committed to supporting Colombia in its pursuit of lasting peace, justice and reconciliation" (Dujarric 2025).

Türk pointed out the importance of the Government's action to comply with the sanctions. He stressed that "it is now up to the Government to take action so the legal, budgetary, security and administrative conditions are in place to ensure that the ensuing penalties are effectively enforced and that accountability is fully embedded in the system" (Mishra 2025).

Nonetheless, the effectiveness of the sanctions could be impacted by the United States' successful effort to remove the supervision of the proper sanctions from the UN Verification Mission's mandate. On October 31, 2025, the Security Council decided, with 13 votes in favour and two abstentions (United States and Russia), that the Mission would no longer monitor the restorative sanctions (United Nations 2025). This decision was influenced by the US position that the Mission had exceeded its original scope and that the country did not want to yield on its policies concerning peace and security in favour of a flawed peace process.

Several countries supported the resolution but spoke in favour of maintaining the monitoring functions, among them, China and Russia (United Nations 2025). A few days later, the JEP asserted that this measure would not affect the verification and monitoring of the sanctions, as the SeRVR and the Executive Secretariat had the institutional capacity of undertaking these tasks (Jurisdicción Especial para la Paz [@JEP_Colombia] 2025).

Despite this setback, on November 6, 2025, the UN High Commissioner for Human Rights confirmed that this office would assume the monitoring functions previously held by the UN Verification Mission (Stacey 2025). In other words, this development shows that the international support for the JEP remains robust, thereby sustaining its international legitimacy. Indeed, the recently appointed UN Verification

Mission chief, Miroslav Jenča, expressed that the UN's commitment remains intact and that the mandate's adjustments do not represent diminished international support (Stacey 2025).

7.4.3 Obedience

The two sentences handed down by the SeRVR in September 2025 may also significantly impact the perception of obedience towards the JEP's rulings. Several experts and public agencies have manifested that complying with the proper sanctions is a complex task and have questioned whether full compliance is feasible. These sanctions require substantial financial resources, sustained inter-institutional cooperation and greater clarity concerning their retributive component, among other challenges. In seeking to implement sanctions effectively, the JEP and the State as a whole are placing the JEP's legitimacy at stake. In this context, compliance with the rulings is questioned more than ever.

Paola Molano, Director of the Transitional Justice Research line at the think-and-do tank Dejusticia, underlined that the legitimacy of the JEP's sentences ultimately hinges on its effective implementation (2025). In turn, the effectiveness of the sanctions is shaped by three factors: (1) the restriction of liberty component; (2) the design and implementation of the restorative projects; and (3) the social credibility of the sanctions, which itself depends on the success of the first two elements. In a preliminary evaluation it seems that this effectiveness cannot be taken for granted.

Regarding the first condition, as described before, the restrictions on the liberties and rights of the former members of the last FARC-EP Secretariat could have been more specific. The public does not know in which municipalities these convicted individuals are required to live, according to what criteria these locations are determined and whether these places of residence may change as projects progress. Furthermore, the protocols for authorising a change of place of residence remain undefined, as the sentences granted a three-month period to create them. It was expected that the ruling would establish clearer conditions regarding the verification and monitoring of the sanctions and the perimeters of the restriction of liberty. These elements are essential for strengthening obedience and assessing the credibility of the retributive component, precisely the most controversial element of the JEP's sanctions.

According to Molano, the Peace Agreement stipulated that the restorative projects be guided by the principle of holistic integration. However, the two sentences fail to fully integrate the sanctions into existing public policies and institutional frameworks. Instead, they order restorative projects from scratch, without relying on existing mechanisms. For instance, they do not take into account the Development Plans created under the Peace Agreement for the municipalities most affected by the conflict, nor do they incorporate the Collective Reparation Plans led by the Unity for Victims. Rather, each ruling contains more than 100 individual orders directed at particular public agencies, requiring them to expand their service provision to the victims. This option, Molano stressed, disperses State action, making the implementation of the sanctions less feasible, and places significant pressure on the public budget, particularly in 2025, when Colombia's fiscal deficit has increased.

Molano concludes that criticisms arising from procedural delays and implementation challenges can only be addressed through the rigorous execution of the sanctions. If they are not fulfilled promptly, there is a risk of reinforcing the perception that sanctions lack effectiveness. Compliance already appears to be difficult, as many projects are in a design stage and require substantial time and funds to be implemented. As a result, the proper execution of the retributive component becomes even more crucial, since having only sentences perceived as merely symbolic would seriously erode the victims' trust and the purposes of transitional justice.

In a separate analysis, Paula Andrea Valencia, a researcher on transitional justice at Dejusticia, and Mateo Merchán, a Colombian scholar and expert on the JEP, emphasised that it is crucial for the JEP to issue orders that are feasible (Valencia and Merchán Duque 2025). They stressed that the JEP should have in mind that the execution of the sentences relies on governmental action. This situation recalls Gibson and Caldeira' observation that courts have neither the power of the sword nor the purse, as discussed in Sect. 4.2.3.

Moreover, victim reparation is a responsibility of the State as a whole; the JEP is not the sole institution in charge of it. Judicial orders should be articulated with existing policies and institutions. Otherwise, the JEP risks promising outcomes that it cannot deliver.

Along similar lines, the Office of the Comptroller General of Colombia, which oversees public finances, warned that the JEP still needs 500,000 million pesos to fund its decisions. However, it remains unclear whether they are included in the National Budget (Casanova 2025).

7.5 Conclusion

The JEP's two first sentences have had an impact on its legitimacy. Many audiences seem less satisfied with these decisions than with the previous rulings issued to develop the macro-cases. In many cases, the sanctions failed to meet expectations and were instead perceived as symbols of impunity. In particular, the retributive component, especially in the FARC-EP's case, has not been regarded as sufficiently robust to satisfy prevailing demands for justice.

After a considerable period without definitive rulings, society has found it increasingly difficult to perceive the benefits of transitional justice in terms of peace, particularly as public security has deteriorated in recent years. Procedural delays have eroded the JEP's authority as a peace-building institution.

From a restorative perspective, many victims reported that they do not feel adequately compensated in relation to the harms they experienced. In some cases, sanctions have been perceived as too lenient and unfair, whereas the content and feasibility of restorative projects remain unclear.

The sentences have also reinforced the mistrust of audiences that have opposed the JEP since its inception and may have strengthened narratives portraying the JEP as synonymous with impunity.

At this stage, the weight of the legitimacy factors seems to skew towards the obedience component. The JEP could mitigate these perceptions of injustice by implementing the sanctions with effectiveness and rigour. In doing so, it faces the obstacle of operationalising restorative projects without having either the power of the sword (the control of State action as a whole) or the purse (financial resources), and after the UN Verification Mission was excluded from the monitoring functions.

These developments illustrate that the weight of legitimacy factors changes over time. Even though handing down definitive rulings is still a very important component for a transitional justice mechanism with a limited mandate, progressively, compliance with the JEP's rulings is becoming more important and expectations across audiences are increasing.

Undoubtedly, the JEP's efforts to fulfil its objectives and meet expectations have been substantial. Since its early days, it has developed transitional justice procedures largely from scratch, delivered rulings that have clarified many atrocities and contributed to reshaping public narratives around some of the most painful crimes committed during

Colombia's internal armed conflict. The JEP has sought to include both victims and perpetrators in its processes, offered plural and triangulated accounts of the truth, and attempted to build an institutional framework to fulfil proper sanctions, among many other results that are described throughout this book.

At the same time, the JEP's legitimacy has fluctuated, as the institution, its operation and multiple external factors have evolved. As proper sanctions have been imposed, the JEP's social authority has increasingly hinged on compliance with its decisions and the effective enforcement of liberty restrictions. Gradually the role of other public institutions and the capacity of the Colombian State as a whole have become more decisive for the JEP's authority to issue decisions and operate.

As a now established Court, the JEP's legitimacy is becoming deeply connected with its effectiveness. The effectiveness in solving the judicial situation for non-most responsible individuals, in promptly sanctioning those most responsible for the victimisation macro-patterns, in ensuring meaningful victim participation in its procedures, in investigating patterns of macro-criminality and in properly implementing sanctions in ways that demonstrate the potential seriousness and benefits of restorative justice. While outcomes are difficult to predict, the hope is that this book offers conceptual tools to analyse the JEP's legitimacy at any time, provides insights for improving its operations, and honours the efforts made by so many who have worked to build peace in Colombia. Nowadays, it is not clear whether the JEP will be the first of many Peace Tribunals to come in a world more affected by wars, or the last of its kind. But certainly, it is proof of a consistent, collective project to address the past and shape a more peaceful future.

References

Álvaro Uribe Vélez [@AlvaroUribeVel]. 2025. "Con el nefasto acuerdo de La Habana la JEP era innecesaria, habría bastado una declaración ante un notario y una supervisión de la justicia. Militares han declarado delitos no cometidos para garantizar su libertad, esta trampa a nuestros soldados fue advertida sin receptividad." Tweet. Twitter, September 17. https://x.com/AlvaroUribeVel/status/1968339201964871752.

Casanova, Gabriela. 2025. "¿Qué está pasando en la JEP?: Contraloría alerta falta de recursos para financiar las decisiones del tribunal." Cambio, August

28. https://cambiocolombia.com/poder/articulo/2025/8/contraloria-alerta-falta-de-recursos-para-financiar-las-decisiones-de-la-jep-que-esta-pasando/.

Clara Rojas [@CLARAROJASG]. 2025. "Esta sentencia no tiene proporcionalidad con la inmensidad del daño causado a 21.800 víctimas. Tampoco hay verdad total, lo cual permitía sanciones más altas, como lo prevee la ley. Les mantienen derechos politicos, tampoco hay ningún tipo de reparación directa, ni económica ni." Tweet. Twitter, September 16. https://x.com/CLARAROJASG/status/1968042030455463962.

De la Calle Lombana, Humberto. 2025. "Desmemoria." Text. ELESPECTADOR.COM, September 28. https://www.elespectador.com/opinion/columnistas/humberto-de-la-calle/desmemoria/.

Dujarric, Stéphane. 2025. "Statement Attributable to the Spokesperson for the Secretary-General - on Colombia [Scroll down for Spanish Version] | Secretary-General | United Nations." September 17. https://www.un.org/sg/en/content/sg/statements/2025-09-17/statement-attributable-the-spokesperson-for-the-secretary-general-colombia-scroll-down-for-spanish-version.

Gómez, Licsa. 2025. "Víctimas calificaron como 'burla', 'vergüenza' y 'traición' la primera sentencia de la JEP contra excomandantes de las Farc." Infobae, September 16. https://www.infobae.com/colombia/2025/09/16/victimas-calificaron-como-burla-verguenza-y-traicion-la-primera-sentencia-de-la-jep-contra-excomandantes-de-las-farc/.

JEP Press Office. 2025. "El último Secretariado de las Farc-EP recibe la máxima Sanción Propia por los secuestros. Trabajará por 8 años en búsqueda de desaparecidas, acción contra minas, medio ambiente y reparación simbólica." Jurisdicción Especial para la Paz, September 16. https://www.jep.gov.co:443/Sala-de-Prensa/Paginas/-la-jep-dicta-su-primera-sentencia-por-los-secuestros-el-ultimo-secretariado-de-las-farc-ep-es-condenado-con-la-maxima-san.aspx.

Juanita Goebertus [@JuanitaGoe]. 2025. "La @JEP_Colombia cocondenó al último Secretariado de la antiguas FARC por la política de secuestro como crimen de lesa humanidad y de guerra. Es un paso fundamental para hacer justicia y satisfacer a las víctimas. 🧵👇Pero nos preocupa la falta de claridad sobre las sanciones." Tweet. Twitter, September 16. https://x.com/JuanitaGoe/status/1967979722383692144.

Jurisdicción Especial para la Paz [@JEP_Colombia]. 2025. " 🔹Aunque la Misión de Verificación de la ONU ya no hará seguimiento directo a las sanciones restaurativas de la JEP, el respaldo internacional a la justicia transicional en Colombia permanece intacto. 🌍Países como Reino Unido y Dinamarca reafirmaron ante el Consejo de https://t.co/MjBAhmc4dQ." Tweet. Twitter, November 3. https://x.com/JEP_Colombia/status/1985350565010821526.

La Silla Vacía, dir. 2025. *Lo Que Viene Después de Las Sentencias de La JEP a Las Farc y a Los Militares Por Falsos Positivos*. 50:55. https://www.youtube.com/watch?v=14NvqwHlf7c.

León, Juanita. 2025. "JEP vs. Farc: una sentencia histórica y un sapo difícil de tragar." *La Silla Vacía*, September 17. https://www.lasillavacia.com/silla-nacional/jep-vs-farc-una-sentencia-historica-y-un-sapo-dificil-de-tragar/.

María Jimena Duzán, dir. 2025. *Así van a Operan Las Sanciones de La JEP Contra Las FARC Por El Delito Del Secuestro*. 42:33. https://www.youtube.com/watch?v=NUbKnK1ze6A.

Mesa Loaiza, Paulina. 2025. "Sentencias de la JEP: las voces de las víctimas de secuestro por las extintas Farc." Text. ELESPECTADOR.COM, September 21. https://www.elespectador.com/colombia-20/jep-y-desaparecidos/sentencias-de-la-jep-las-voces-de-las-victimas-de-secuestro-por-las-extintas-farc/.

Mishra, Vibhu. 2025. "UN Hails Colombia's First Convictions under Transitional Justice Measures as 'Crucial Milestone' | UN News." September 17. https://news.un.org/en/story/2025/09/1165871.

Molano, Paola. 2025. "La legitimidad de las sentencias de la JEP dependerá de su cumplimiento." *La Silla Vacía*, September 23. https://www.lasillavacia.com/red-de-expertos/red-de-la-paz/la-legitimidad-de-las-sentencias-de-la-jep-dependera-de-su-cumplimiento/.

Osorio, Camila. 2025. "Las víctimas del secuestro critican la primera condena de la JEP contra las FARC: 'La sensación de impunidad es rampante.'" El País América Colombia, September 17. https://elpais.com/america-colombia/2025-09-17/las-victimas-del-secuestro-critican-la-primera-condena-de-la-jep-contra-las-farc-la-sensacion-de-impunidad-es-rampante.html.

Rojas, Gabriel. 2025. "Primeras sentencias restaurativas por crímenes atroces: la justicia transicional colombiana en acción - Agenda Estado de Derecho." Región Andina. *Agenda Estado de Derecho*, November 6. https://agendaestadodederecho.com/primeras-sentencias-restaurativas-por-crimenes-atroces/.

Santos, Francisco. 2025. "Teníamos razón." Semana.com Últimas Noticias de Colombia y el Mundo, September 20. https://www.semana.com/opinion/articulo/teniamos-razon/202535/.

Section of Acknowledgement of Responsibility and Truth. 2025a. *Sentence TP-SeRVR-RC-ST-001-2025*. https://relatoria.jep.gov.co//documentos/providencias/4/2/Sentencia_TP-SeRVR-RC-ST-001-2025_16-septiembre-2025.pdf.

Section of Acknowledgement of Responsibility and Truth. 2025b. *Sentence TP-SeRVR-RC-ST-002*.

Stacey, Diego. 2025. "La justicia transicional de Colombia conserva el apoyo de la ONU pese a las reticencias del Consejo de Seguridad." El País América Colombia, November 6. https://elpais.com/america-colombia/2025-11-06/la-justicia-transicional-de-colombia-conserva-el-apoyo-de-la-onu-pese-a-las-reticencias-del-consejo-de-seguridad.html.

Torres Lasso, Juan Diego. 2025. "Familiares Dividen Sus Posiciones Frente a Las Dos Sentencias de La JEP Contra 12 Militares y 7 exFarc." *El Tiempo*, September 20. https://web.archive.org/web/20251009202109/https://www.eltiempo.com/justicia/jep-colombia/familiares-dividen-sus-posiciones-frente-a-las-dos-sentencias-de-la-jep-contra-12-militares-y-7-exfarc-3492586.

United Nations. 2025. "Colombia: El Consejo de Seguridad reduce el mandato de la Misión de la ONU en ese país | Noticias ONU." Paz y Seguridad, October 31. https://news.un.org/es/story/2025/10/1540672.

Valencia, Paula Andrea, and Mateo Merchán Duque. 2025. "Las sentencias de la JEP ya están, ¿pero se pueden cumplir?" *La Silla Vacía*, October 16. https://www.lasillavacia.com/red-de-expertos/red-de-la-paz/las-sentencias-de-la-jep-ya-estan-pero-se-pueden-cumplir/.

Bibliography

Allioui, Samira. 2020. "Legitimacy and International Courts." *International Journal for Court Administration* 11 (1). https://doi.org/10.36745/ijca.288.

Álvaro Uribe Vélez [@AlvaroUribeVel]. 2023. "Duele y mortifica que hubieran negado falsos positivos, les creímos, y ahora los aceptan; incluso la Fundación de Herbin Hoyos, qepd, defendió un caso de Dabeiba, anterior a mi Gbno. Y apoyamos esa defensa. Los cometidos durante mi Gbno mancharon la Seguridad Democrática que." Tweet. Twitter, June 29. https://twitter.com/AlvaroUribeVel/status/1674214007962583040.

Álvaro Uribe Vélez [@AlvaroUribeVel]. 2025. "Con el nefasto acuerdo de La Habana la JEP era innecesaria, habría bastado una declaración ante un notario y una supervisión de la justicia. Militares han declarado delitos no cometidos para garantizar su libertad, esta trampa a nuestros soldados fue advertida sin receptividad." Tweet. Twitter, September 17. https://x.com/AlvaroUribeVel/status/1968339201964871752.

Ámbito Jurídico. 2019. "Detalle de las razones de Duque al objetar la Ley Estatutaria de la JEP." Ámbito Jurídico, March 11. https://www.ambitojuridico.com/noticias/general/administrativo-y-contratacion/detalle-de-las-razones-de-duque-al-objetar-la-ley.

Anna Myriam Roccatello and Gabriel Rojas. 2020. *A Mixed Approach to International Crimes: The Retributive and Restorative Justice Procedures of Colombia's Special Jurisdiction for Peace*. International Center for Transitional Justice. https://www.ictj.org/sites/default/files/ICTJ_Report_Colombia_MixedProcedures.pdf.

N. Zuluaga Afanador, *The Sociological Legitimacy of the Special Jurisdiction for Peace of Colombia*, St Antony's Series, https://doi.org/10.1007/978-3-032-21912-1

AP News. 2021. "Colombia: expresidente Uribe declara sobre falsos positivos." AP News, August 16. https://apnews.com/article/noticias-c2cf010e95c0e4836732aeab28a5da6d.

Auto 019 de 2021 (Special Jurisdiction for Peace January 26, 2021). https://www.jep.gov.co/Sala-de-Prensa/Documents/CASO%2001%20TOMA%20DE%20REHENES/Auto%20No.%2019%20de%202021.pdf?csf=1&e=16bYs0.

BBC News Mundo. 2010. "BBC Mundo - América Latina - Corte Constitucional de Colombia dice 'no' a la reelección de Álvaro Uribe." British Broadcasting Corporation, February 27. 10/02/100226_2238_uribe_reeleccion_colombia_constitucional_irm.shtml.

BBC News Mundo. 2016a. "Colombia: el Congreso aprueba el nuevo acuerdo de paz con las FARC y las divisiones se trasladan a las presidenciales de 2018." *BBC News Mundo*, December 1. https://www.bbc.com/mundo/noticias-america-latina-38165978.

BBC News Mundo. 2016b. "Colombia: ganó el 'No' en el plebiscito por los acuerdos de paz con las FARC." *BBC News Mundo*, October 2. https://www.bbc.com/mundo/noticias-america-latina-37537187.

BBC News Mundo. 2019. "La Corte Constitucional de Colombia rechaza las objeciones de Duque a la polémica ley que juzga a los involucrados en el conflicto armado." *BBC News Mundo*, May 30. https://www.bbc.com/mundo/noticias-america-latina-48453600.

BBC News Mundo. 2021. "Las disidencias de las FARC confirman la muerte del guerrillero colombiano Jesús Santrich en territorio venezolano." *BBC News Mundo*, May 18. https://www.bbc.com/mundo/noticias-america-latina-57165018.

Beetham, David. 2002. *The Legitimation of Power*. 5th print. Issues in Political Theory. Macmillan.

Beetham, David. 2013. *The Legitimation of Power*. 2nd ed. Political Analysis (Palgrave Macmillan (Firm)). Palgrave Macmillan.

Bennett, Andrew, and Jeffrey T. Checkel. 2014. "Process Tracing: From Philosophical Roots to Best Practices." In *Process Tracing*, 1st ed., edited by Andrew Bennett and Jeffrey T. Checkel. Cambridge University Press. https://doi.org/10.1017/CBO9781139858472.003.

Bermúdez Liévano, Andrés, ed. 2018. *Los debates de La Habana: una mirada desde adentro*. Fondo de Capital Humano para la Transición Colombiana, Instituto para las Transiciones Integrales (IFIT).

Biblioteca Abierta del Proceso de Paz colombiano. 2021. "BAPP - Biblioteca Abierta del Proceso de Paz colombiano." *¿Cuándo? El proceso de paz en el tiempo*, March 29. https://bapp.com.co/cuando/.

Borda, Fals, Germán Guzmán Orlando, and Eduardo Umaña. 1962. "La Violencia En Colombia." *Bogotá: Tercer Mundo*.

Botero, Sandra. 2020. "Trust in Colombia's Justicia Especial Para La Paz: Experimental Evidence." *Journal of Politics in Latin America* 12 (3): 300–322. https://doi.org/10.1177/1866802X20959509.

Canal Institucional de Colombia. 2020. "Las razones de la CPI para decir que JEP es referente mundial." Canal Institucional TV, November 3. https://www.canalinstitucional.tv/noticias/jep-es-ejemplo-internacional-segun-corte-penal-internacional.

Caracol Radio. 2024. "Así se perdieron 9 decretos con las amnistías para 9.600 exFarc." Caracol Radio, May 6. https://caracol.com.co/2024/05/06/asi-se-perdieron-9-decretos-con-las-amnistias-para-9600-exfarc/.

Casanova, Gabriela. 2025. "¿Qué está pasando en la JEP?: Contraloría alerta falta de recursos para financiar las decisiones del tribunal." Cambio, August 28. https://cambiocolombia.com/poder/articulo/2025/8/contraloria-alerta-falta-de-recursos-para-financiar-las-decisiones-de-la-jep-que-esta-pasando/.

Cindy A. Morales Castillo. 2024. "Exsecretariado de FARC propone 'tribunal de cierre' por presuntos incumplimientos de JEP." Paz y Memoria. *El Espectador*, February 24. https://www.elespectador.com/colombia-20/paz-y-memoria/exsecretariado-de-farc-propondra-a-petro-un-tribunal-de-cierre-que-podria-eliminar-a-la-jep/.

Clara Rojas [@CLARAROJASG]. 2025. "Esta sentencia no tiene proporcionalidad con la inmensidad del daño causado a 21.800 víctimas. Tampoco hay verdad total, lo cual permitía sanciones más altas, como lo prevee la ley. Les mantienen derechos politicos, tampoco hay ningún tipo de reparación directa, ni económica ni." Tweet. Twitter, September 16. https://x.com/CLARAROJASG/status/1968042030455463962.

Cohen, Harlan Grant, Andreas Follesdal, Nienke Grossman, and Geir Ulfstein. 2018. "Legitimacy and International Courts – A Framework." In *Legitimacy and International Courts*, 1st ed., edited by Nienke Grossman, Harlan Grant Cohen, Andreas Follesdal, and Geir Ulfstein. Cambridge University Press. https://doi.org/10.1017/9781108529570.001.

Coicaud, Jean-Marc. 2002. *Legitimacy and Politics: A Contribution to the Study of Political Right and Political Responsibility*. With David Ames Curtis and Cambridge University Press. Cambridge Core. University Press. https://ezproxy-prd.bodleian.ox.ac.uk/login?url=10.1017/CBO9780511490200.

Colombian Government and FARC-EP. 2016. "Peace Agreement 2016." November 26. https://www.peaceagreements.org/wview/1845/Final%20Agreement%20to%20End%20the%20Armed%20Conflict%20and%20Build%20a%20Stable%20and%20Lasting%20Peace.

Congress of the Republic of Colombia. 2017. "Constitutional Reform 1 of 2017." April 4. http://www.secretariasenado.gov.co/senado/basedoc/acto_legislativo_01_2017.html.

Connolly, Christopher K. 2006. "Living on the Past: The Role of Truth Commissions in Post-Conflict Societies and the Case Study of Northern Ireland." *Cornell International Law Journal* 39: 401.

Constitutional Court of Colombia. 2018. "Ruling C-080-18." August 15. https://www.corteconstitucional.gov.co/relatoria/2018/c-080-18.htm.

De la Calle Lombana, Humberto. 2019. *Revelaciones al Final de Una Guerra: Testimonio Del Jefe Negociador Del Gobierno Colombiano En La Habana.* DEBATE.

De la Calle Lombana, Humberto. 2025. "Desmemoria." Text. ELESPECTADOR.COM, September 28. https://www.elespectador.com/opinion/columnistas/humberto-de-la-calle/desmemoria/.

Desjardins, Jeff. 2019. "Mapped: The World's Oldest Democracies." World Economic Forum, August 8. https://www.weforum.org/stories/2019/08/countries-are-the-worlds-oldest-democracies/.

Dujarric, Stéphane. 2025. "Statement Attributable to the Spokesperson for the Secretary-General - on Colombia [Scroll down for Spanish Version] | Secretary-General | United Nations." September 17. https://www.un.org/sg/en/content/sg/statements/2025-09-17/statement-attributable-the-spokesperson-for-the-secretary-general-colombia-scroll-down-for-spanish-version.

Easton, David. 1975. "A Re-Assessment of the Concept of Political Support." *British Journal of Political Science* 5 (4): 435–57. https://doi.org/10.1017/S0007123400008309.

El Colombiano. 2010. "La de Uribe, una histórica popularidad." El Colombiano, August 5. https://www.elcolombiano.com/historico/la_de_uribe_una_historica_popularidad-HVEC_99428.

El Espectador. 2020a. "La cuestionable estrategia de campaña del No." Text. ELESPECTADOR.COM, March 24. https://www.elespectador.com/politica/la-cuestionable-estrategia-de-campana-del-no-article-658862/.

El Espectador. 2020b. "Pasados cuatro años del plebiscito que dividió a Colombia." Text. ELESPECTADOR.COM, October 2. https://www.elespectador.com/politica/pasados-cuatro-anos-del-plebiscito-que-dividio-a-colombia-article/.

El Espectador. 2024a. "Corte Constitucional rechaza por segunda vez demanda del exministro Yesid Reyes." Judicial. *El Espectador* (Bogotá), November 1. https://www.elespectador.com/judicial/por-segunda-vez-corte-constitucional-rechazo-demanda-del-exministro-yesid-reyes-noticias-de-hoy/.

El Espectador. 2024b. "El grito de respeto por la JEP que lideran las víctimas de las FARC." Text. ELESPECTADOR.COM, March 10. https://www.elespectador.com/judicial/el-grito-de-respeto-por-la-jep-que-lideran-las-victimas-de-las-farc/.

El País. 2016. "Uribe rechaza el nuevo acuerdo de paz entre el Gobierno y las FARC y pide un nuevo plebiscito." América Colombia. *El País*

(Madrid), November 22. https://elpais.com/internacional/2016/11/22/colombia/1479819217_374727.html.

El País. 2018. "La detención del exlíder de las FARC Jesús Santrich tensa el proceso de paz en Colombia." América Colombia. *El País* (Madrid), April 11. https://elpais.com/internacional/2018/04/10/colombia/1523394661_758627.html.

El País. 2019. "El fiscal de Colombia dimite tras la orden de liberación de un exlíder de las FARC." América Colombia. *El País* (Madrid), May 16. https://elpais.com/internacional/2019/05/15/colombia/1557944015_282644.html.

El País. 2024. "Comienza la justicia restaurativa en Colombia: los antiguos criminales de guerra que siembran bosques." El País América Colombia, April 3. https://elpais.com/america-colombia/2024-04-03/comienza-la-justicia-restaurativa-en-colombia-los-antiguos-criminales-de-guerra-que-siembran-bosques.html.

Ferry, Stephen. 2012. *Violentology: A Manual of the Colombian Conflict*. 1st ed. Umbrage.

Figueroa Cordero, Ronald Javier. 2022. "Relatos de 'Todo Lo Malo': El Caso de Chulavita, Memoria Sobre La Violencia." Universidad de los Andes. http://hdl.handle.net/1992/60723.

Forero-Alba, Sofía, and Juan Carlos Rodríguez-Raga. 2022. "Courting Judicial Legitimacy: An Experimental Study of the Colombian Constitutional Court." In *The Limits of Judicialization*, 1st ed., edited by Sandra Botero, Daniel M. Brinks, and Ezequiel A. Gonzalez-Ocantos. Cambridge University Press. https://doi.org/10.1017/9781009093859.007.

Galtung, Johan. 1969. "Violence, Peace, and Peace Research." *Journal of Peace Research* 6 (3): 167–91. https://doi.org/10.1177/002234336900600301.

Gibson, James L., and Gregory A. Caldeira. 2003. "Defenders of Democracy? Legitimacy, Popular Acceptance, and the South African Constitutional Court." *The Journal of Politics* 65 (1): 1–30. https://doi.org/10.1111/1468-2508.t01-1-00001.

Gibson, James, Gregory Caldeira, and Vanessa Baird. 1998. "On the Legitimacy of National High Courts." *The American Political Science Review* 92 (June): 343. https://doi.org/10.2307/2585668.

Gómez, Gabriel Ignacio. 2022. "Political Conflicts over the JEP: A Sociolegal Perspective." In *Transitional Justice in Colombia: The Special Jurisdiction for Peace [Electronic Resource]*, edited by Kai Ambos and Stefan Peters, with Susann Aboueldahab. Studien Zu Lateinamerika; Volume 44. Nomos. https://directory.doabooks.org/handle/20.500.12854/81931.

Gómez, Licsa. 2025. "Víctimas calificaron como 'burla', 'vergüenza' y 'traición' la primera sentencia de la JEP contra excomandantes de las Farc." Infobae, September 16. https://www.infobae.com/colombia/2025/09/16/victimas-calificaron-como-burla-verguenza-y-traicion-la-primera-sentencia-de-la-jep-contra-excomandantes-de-las-farc/.

Gomez-Suarez, Andrei. 2016. *El triunfo del no: la paradoja emocional detrás del plebiscito*. Paradoja emocional detrás del plebiscito. Icono.

González Ocantos, Ezequiel. 2017. *Shifting Legal Visions: Judicial Change and Human Rights Trials in Latin America*. Cambridge University Press. https://www.cambridge.org/core/books/shifting-legal-visions/CC9D850D90D984A72AA455DC32A8C56D.

Grupo de Memoria Histórica. 2013. *¡Basta ya! Colombia, memorias de guerra y dignidad: informe general*. Segunda edición corregida. Centro Nacional de Memoria Histórica.

Guevara, Carolina. 2011. "Independencia Judicial: El Caso de La Corte Suprema de Justicia Colombiana." *Revista de Derecho*, no. 35: 145–79.

Gutiérrez, Martha. 2022. "La Corte Constitucional frente a la Paz: control al acuerdo de paz de Colombia y su implementación." *Reflexión Política* 24 (50): 50. https://doi.org/10.29375/01240781.4535.

Gutiérrez Sanín, Francisco. 2020. *¿Un nuevo ciclo de la guerra en Colombia?* DEBATE.

Hamber, Brandon. 2002. "Rights and Reasons: Challenges for Truth Recovery in South Africa and Northern Ireland." *Fordham International Law Journal* 26: 1074.

Harvey, William S. 2011. "Strategies for Conducting Elite Interviews." *Qualitative Research* 11 (4): 431–41. https://doi.org/10.1177/1468794111404329.

Infobae. 2021. "'Perdió el plebiscito, es impuesta por las Farc y sesgada': nueva arremetida de Uribe contra la JEP." infobae, March 31. https://www.infobae.com/america/colombia/2021/03/31/perdio-el-plebiscito-es-impuesta-por-las-farc-y-sesgada-nueva-arremetida-de-uribe-contra-la-jep/.

Infobae. 2024. "Álvaro Uribe aseguró que la JEP está en deuda con los soldados: 'Recibieron el trato de ejército de matones.'" infobae, March 5. https://www.infobae.com/colombia/2024/03/05/alvaro-uribe-aseguro-que-la-jep-esta-en-deuda-con-los-soldados-colombianos-recibieron-el-trato-de-ejercito-de-matones/.

Interamerican Court of Human Rights. 2012. *Sentencia Corte IDH Masacre el Mozote Vs El Salvador 2012*. https://corteidh.or.cr/docs/casos/articulos/seriec_252_esp.pdf.

International Criminal Court. 2021. "ICC Prosecutor, Mr Karim A. A. Khan QC, Concludes the Preliminary Examination of the Situation in Colombia with a Cooperation Agreement with the Government Charting the next Stage in Support of Domestic Efforts to Advance Transitional Justice." October 28. https://www.icc-cpi.int/news/icc-prosecutor-mr-karim-khan-qc-concludes-preliminary-examination-situation-colombia.

International Criminal Court. 2024. "Colombia | International Criminal Court." May 13. https://www.icc-cpi.int/colombia.

International Criminal Court Office of the Prosecutor. 2012. *Situation in Colombia - Interim Report*. ICC Office of the Prosecutor. https://www.icc-cpi.int/sites/default/files/2022-09/OTPCOLOMBIAPublicInterimReportNovember2012.pdf.

Invamer. 2024. "Encuesta Invamer Febrero 2024." February. https://caracoltv.brightspotcdn.com/2c/ae/5173738245abb2e043034a0c173a/encuesta-invamer-poll-febrero-2024.pdf.

Iván Orozco Abad. 2020. "Sobre Algunos Desafíos Conceptuales y de Legitimidad de La JEP." In *La JEP Vista Por Sus Jueces (2018–2019)*, edited by Jurisdicción Especial para la Paz. Jurisdicción Especial para la Paz. https://www.jep.gov.co/Documents/LA%20JEP%20VISTA%20POR%20SUS%20JUEVES.pdf.

JEP Government Board. 2024. "Acuerdo 7 de 2024." February 16. https://www.jep.gov.co/organosgobierno/Acuerdo%20AOG%20007%20de%202024.pdf.

JEP Press Office. 2019a. "La Sección de Revisión de la JEP aplica la garantía de no extradición a Seuxis Paucias Hernández." May 15. https://www.jep.gov.co:443/Sala-de-Prensa/Paginas/LA-SECCI%C3%93N-DE-REVISI%C3%93N-DE-LA-JEP-APLICA-LA-GARANT%C3%8DA-DE-NO-EXTRADICI%C3%93N-A-SEUXIS-PAUCIAS-HERN%C3%81NDEZ-SOLARTE.aspx.

JEP Press Office. 2019b. "Víctimas podrán participar en versiones de la Sala de Reconocimiento de la JEP." June 6. https://www.jep.gov.co:443/Sala-de-Prensa/Paginas/V%C3%ADctimas-podr%C3%A1n-participar-en-versiones-de-la-Sala-de-Reconocimiento-de-la-JEP.aspx.

JEP Press Office. 2020. "Tres historias para comprender los TOAR en la JEP." October 19. https://www.jep.gov.co:443/Sala-de-Prensa/Paginas/Tres-historias-para-comprender-los-TOAR-en-la-JEP.aspx.

JEP Press Office. 2023a. "JEP ha imputado a 148 máximos responsables de crímenes de guerra y lesa humanidad en el conflicto armado." December 5. https://www.jep.gov.co:443/Sala-de-Prensa/Paginas/-jep-ha-imputado-a-148-maximos-responsables-de-crimenes-de-guerra-y-lesa-humanidad-en-el-conflicto-armado.aspx.

JEP Press Office. 2023b. "JEP pide a Fiscalía que investigue conductas de antiguos servidores del ente acusador." March 6. https://www.jep.gov.co:443/Sala-de-Prensa/Paginas/jep-pide-a-fiscal%C3%ADa-que-investigue-conductas-de-antiguos-servidores-del-ente-acusador.aspx.

JEP Press Office. 2023c. "La JEP y la Fiscalía de la Corte Penal Internacional profundizan cooperación." June 6. https://www.jep.gov.co:443/Sala-de-Prensa/Paginas/la-jep-y-la-fiscalia-de-la-corte-penal-internacional-profundizan-cooperacion.aspx.

JEP Press Office. 2024a. "JEP comunica decretos de amnistía a más de 9.600 firmantes del Acuerdo Final de Paz." February 21. https://www.jep.gov.co:443/Sala-de-Prensa/Paginas/-jep-comunica-decretos-de-amnistia-a-mas-de-9600-firmantes-del-acuerdo-final-de-paz.aspx.

JEP Press Office. 2024b. "JEP fortalece su mandato con Acuerdo de Complementariedad firmado entre el Gobierno y la Fiscalía de la Corte Penal Internacional." April 27. https://www.jep.gov.co:443/Sala-de-Prensa/Paginas/-jep-fortalece-su-mandato-con-acuerdo-de-complementariedad-firmado-entre-el-gobierno-y-la-fiscalia-de-la-corte-penal-intern.aspx.

JEP Press Office. 2025. "El último Secretariado de las Farc-EP recibe la máxima Sanción Propia por los secuestros. Trabajará por 8 años en búsqueda de desaparecidas, acción contra minas, medio ambiente y reparación simbólica." Jurisdicción Especial para la Paz, September 16. https://www.jep.gov.co:443/Sala-de-Prensa/Paginas/-la-jep-dicta-su-primera-sentencia-por-los-secuestros-el-ultimo-secretariado-de-las-farc-ep-es-condenado-con-la-maxima-san.aspx.

Juanita Goebertus [@JuanitaGoe]. 2025. "La @JEP_Colombia cocondenó al último Secretariado de la antiguas FARC por la política de secuestro como crimen de lesa humanidad y de guerra. Es un paso fundamental para hacer justicia y satisfacer a las víctimas. 🧑‍⚖️👇Pero nos preocupa la falta de claridad sobre las sanciones." Tweet. Twitter, September 16. https://x.com/JuanitaGoe/status/1967979722383692144.

Jurisdicción Especial para la Paz. 2025a. "Caso 01: Toma de rehenes, graves privaciones de la libertad y otros crímenes concurrentes cometidos por las Farc-EP." June 2. https://www.jep.gov.co/macrocasos/caso01.html.

Jurisdicción Especial para la Paz. 2025b. "Caso 03: Asesinatos y desapariciones forzadas presentados como bajas en combate por agentes del Estado." June 2. https://www.jep.gov.co/macrocasos/caso03.html.

Jurisdicción Especial para la Paz. 2025c. "Caso 04: Situación territorial de la región de Urabá." June 2. https://www.jep.gov.co/macrocasos/caso04.html.

Jurisdicción Especial para la Paz. 2025d. "Caso 09: Crímenes no amnistiables cometidos contra Pueblos y Territorios Étnicos en el marco del conflicto armado colombiano." June 2. https://www.jep.gov.co/macrocasos/caso09.html.

Jurisdicción Especial para la Paz. 2025e. "Caso 10: Crímenes no amnistiables cometidos por las extintas Farc-EP en el marco del conflicto armado colombiano." June 2. https://www.jep.gov.co/macrocasos/caso10.html.

Jurisdicción Especial para la Paz. 2025f. "Caso 11: Violencia basada en género, violencia sexual, violencia reproductiva, y otros crímenes cometidos por prejuicio basados en la orientación sexual, la expresión y/o identidad de género diversa en el marco del conflicto armado colombiano." June 2. https://www.jep.gov.co/macrocasos/caso11.html.

Jurisdicción Especial para la Paz. 2025g. "Response to Freedom of Information Request." Jurisdicción Especial para la Paz, May 2.

Jurisdicción Especial para la Paz [@JEP_Colombia]. 2025. " 🔹Aunque la Misión de Verificación de la ONU ya no hará seguimiento directo a las sanciones restaurativas de la JEP, el respaldo internacional a la justicia transicional en Colombia permanece intacto. 🌍Países como Reino Unido y Dinamarca reafirmaron ante el Consejo de https://t.co/MjBAhmc4dQ." Tweet. Twitter, November 3. https://x.com/JEP_Colombia/status/1985350565010821526.

Justice for Colombia [@JFColombia]. 2021. "During today's national strike protesters remember the 6,402 people killed by the Colombian Army in the 2000s. The Army offered false jobs to young people in poor neighbourhoods before murdering them and dressing them as guerrillas to increase their combat figures. #ParoNacional https://t.co/jRselQAWkr." Tweet. Twitter, April 28. https://twitter.com/JFColombia/status/1387481893139099651.

Justice Subcommission of the 2016 Colombian Peace Agreement. 2015. "Subcomisión de Justicia. Bases Compartidas." Biblioteca Abierta del Proceso de Paz colombiano, July 27. https://bapp.com.co/archivos/1.01.0917.pdf.

Kawulich, Barbara B. 2005. "Participant Observation as a Data Collection Method." *Forum: Qualitative Social Research / Qualitative Sozialforschung* 6 (2): 1–22. Business Source Ultimate.

Kutnjak Ivković, Sanja, and John Hagan. 2017. "The Legitimacy of International Courts: Victims' Evaluations of the ICTY and Local Courts in Bosnia and Herzegovina." *European Journal of Criminology* (London, England) 14 (2): 200–220. https://doi.org/10.1177/1477370816649625.

La Silla Vacía. 2024. "Colombia lanzará política de cooperación con la Corte Penal Internacional." La Silla Vacía, April 25. http://www.lasillavacia.com/en-vivo/colombia-lanzara-politica-de-cooperacion-con-la-corte-penal-internacional/.

La Silla Vacía, dir. 2025. *Lo Que Viene Después de Las Sentencias de La JEP a Las Farc y a Los Militares Por Falsos Positivos*. 50:55. https://www.youtube.com/watch?v=14NvqwHlf7c.

La Silla Vacía [@lasillavacia]. 2024. "En una carta a @petrogustavo, exmiembros del último Secretariado de las extintas Farc aseguran que la @JEP_Colombia está incumpliendo el Acuerdo de Paz. La crítica que ocurre el mismo día que llega el Consejo de Seguridad de @ONU_es, que es garante del Acuerdo de 2016. Va 🧵. https://t.co/0ehqM4eR8v." Tweet. Twitter, February 7. https://twitter.com/lasillavacia/status/1755293947847438566.

León, Juanita. 2025. "JEP vs. Farc: una sentencia histórica y un sapo difícil de tragar." *La Silla Vacía*, September 17. https://www.lasillavacia.com/silla-nacional/jep-vs-farc-una-sentencia-historica-y-un-sapo-dificil-de-tragar/.

Leongómez, Eduardo Pizarro. 2015. "Una Lectura Múltiple y Pluralista de La Historia." *Contribución al Entendimiento Del Conflicto Armado En Colombia*, 3–94.

Liévano, Andrés Bermúdez. 2024. "El pecado original interno de la JEP de Colombia." *JusticeInfo.net*, March 1. https://www.justiceinfo.net/es/129032-el-pecado-original-interno-de-la-jep-de-colombia.html.

Lupu, Yonatan. 2013. "International Judicial Legitimacy: Lessons from National Courts." *Theoretical Inquiries in Law* 14 (2). https://doi.org/10.1515/til-2013-022.

Maria del Pilar Bahamón and Harvey Danilo Suárez. 2020. "Legitimidad Por Vía de Juridicidad: Narrativas En Disputa Sobre La Jurisdicción Especial Para La Paz Como Mecanismo de Justicia Restaurativa En Entornos de Impunidad y Polarización." In *La JEP Vista Por Sus Jueces (2018–2019)*.

María Jimena Duzán, dir. 2025. *Así van a Operan Las Sanciones de La JEP Contra Las FARC Por El Delito Del Secuestro*. 42:33. https://www.youtube.com/watch?v=NUbKnK1ze6A.

Mauricio Albarracín Caballero [@malbarracin]. 2021. "#DiarioDeLaProtesta conúmero 6402 se ha convertido en un símbolo de las protestas en Colombia. Este número señala las ejecuciones extrajudiciales que @JEP_Colombia está investigando. Este número se puede ver en muchas partes de la ciudad pero ayer fue instalado en los Héroes https://t.co/7S8mhVqD0b." Tweet. Twitter, May 13. https://twitter.com/malbarracin/status/1392788404547510276.

Mauricio Villamil. 2025. "Corte Constitucional analiza demanda que cuestiona ampliación de investigados por parte de la JEP con la 'Senit 5.'" Colombia. *Infobae*, May 6. https://www.infobae.com/colombia/2025/05/06/corte-constitucional-analiza-demanda-que-cuestiona-ampliacion-de-investigados-por-parte-de-la-jep-con-la-senit-5/.

Mayans-Hermida, Beatriz E. Barbora Holá, and Catrien Bijleveld. 2023. "Between Impunity and Justice? Exploring Stakeholders' Perceptions of Colombia's Special Sanctions (Sanciones Propias) for International Crimes." *International Journal of Transitional Justice*, May 19, ijad009. https://doi.org/10.1093/ijtj/ijad009.

Melo, Jorge Orlando. 2021. *Colombia: una historia mínima: una mirada integral al país*. Crítica.

Merchán Duque, Mateo. 2019. "Historia Del Proceso de Configuración Normativa de La Herramienta de 'Contexto' En El Sistema de Justicia y Paz: La

Tensión Entre La Legitimidad Para Las Víctimas y La Eficiencia Del Sistema." Pontificia Universidad Javeriana. http://hdl.handle.net/10554/45216 La - Spanish.

Mesa Loaiza, Paulina. 2025. "Sentencias de la JEP: las voces de las víctimas de secuestro por las extintas Farc." Text. ELESPECTADOR.COM, September 21. https://www.elespectador.com/colombia-20/jep-y-desaparecidos/sentencias-de-la-jep-las-voces-de-las-victimas-de-secuestro-por-las-extintas-farc/.

Michalowski, Sabine, Michael Cruz Rodríguez, and Hobeth Martínez Carrillo. 2020. *¿A quiénes sancionar? máximos responsables y participación determinante en la Jurisdicción Especial para la Paz*. Documentos Dejusticia 61. Dejusticia.

Mishra, Vibhu. 2025. "UN Hails Colombia's First Convictions under Transitional Justice Measures as 'Crucial Milestone' | UN News." September 17. https://news.un.org/en/story/2025/09/1165871.

Molano, Paola. 2025. "La legitimidad de las sentencias de la JEP dependerá de su cumplimiento." *La Silla Vacía*, September 23. https://www.lasillavacia.com/red-de-expertos/red-de-la-paz/la-legitimidad-de-las-sentencias-de-la-jep-dependera-de-su-cumplimiento/.

National Government of Colombia and FARC-EP. 2012. "Acuerdo General Para La Terminación Del Conflicto y La Construcción de Una Paz Estable y Duradera." Biblioteca Abierta del Proceso de Paz colombiano, August 26. https://bapp.com.co/archivos/1.03.0058.pdf.

Nelson, Thomas E., Rosalee A. Clawson, and Zoe M. Oxley. 1997. "Media Framing of a Civil Liberties Conflict and Its Effect on Tolerance." *American Political Science Review* 91 (3): 567–83. https://doi.org/10.2307/2952075.

Olsen, Tricia D., Leigh A. Payne, and Andrew G. Reiter. 2010. *Transitional Justice in Balance: Comparing Processes, Weighing Efficacy*. U.S. Institute of Peace.

Osorio, Camila. 2025. "Las víctimas del secuestro critican la primera condena de la JEP contra las FARC: 'La sensación de impunidad es rampante.'" El País América Colombia, September 17. https://elpais.com/america-colombia/2025-09-17/las-victimas-del-secuestro-critican-la-primera-condena-de-la-jep-contra-las-farc-la-sensacion-de-impunidad-es-rampante.html.

Ospina-Pedraza, Ana María, Farid Samir Benavides-Vanegas, and Julián Darío Bonilla-Montenegro. 2023. "Keys to Interpreting the International Cooperation of the EU for the Special Jurisdiction for Peace." In *European Union Support for Colombia's Peace Process*, edited by Karlos Pérez De Armiño. Rethinking Peace and Conflict Studies. Springer Nature Switzerland. https://doi.org/10.1007/978-3-031-24797-2_10.

Paola Molano Ayala [@pmolanoayala]. 2024a. "La carta de @ComunesCoL al Presidente sobre la @JEP_Colombia, revela varias cosas preocupantes y urgentes de lado y lado 🧵." Tweet. Twitter, February 7. https://twitter.com/pmolanoayala/status/1755319474075345205.

Paola Molano Ayala [@pmolanoayala]. 2024b. "La decisión de la @JEP_Colombia de nombrar 36 magistrados auxiliares parece escandalosa, teniendo en cuenta que, con arandelas, son salarios de 37 millones de pesos. Además de esto, la decisión da lugar a, al menos, dos discusiones 🧵." Tweet. Twitter, February 5. https://twitter.com/pmolanoayala/status/1754328356038857146.

Pardo Rodriguez, Santiago. 2020. "A Second Chance on Earth: Understanding the Selection Process of the Judges of the Colombian Special Jurisdiction for Peace." *Notre Dame Journal of International & Comparative Law* 10: 209.

Partido COMUNES [@ComunesCoL]. 2024. "¿Por qué hablamos de 'descarrilamiento' de la #JEP? A 7 años de la firma del Acuerdo de paz, este es el avance de la jurisdicción ⬇🧵https://t.co/zFIdgoD6C4." Tweet. Twitter, April 18. https://twitter.com/ComunesCoL/status/1780984818773188673.

Payne, Leigh A., Gabriel Pereira, and Laura Bernal-Bermúdez. 2020. *Transitional Justice and Corporate Accountability from Below: Deploying Archimedes' Lever*. Cambridge University Press. Cambridge Core. https://doi.org/10.1017/9781108564564.

Pianigiani, Ottorino. 1907. *Vocabolario etimologico della lingua italiana*. In *Vocabolario etimologico della lingua italiana*. Società editrice Dante Alighieri di Albrighi, Segati. https://www.etimo.it/?term=legittimo.

Pion-Berlin, David. 1994. "To Prosecute or to Pardon? Human Rights Decisions in the Latin American Southern Cone." *Human Rights Quarterly* 16 (1): 105. https://doi.org/10.2307/762413.

Rebecca Brubaker. 2020. "The UN Security Council and Transitional Justice: Colombia." *United Nations University - Centre for Policy Research*, August. https://i.unu.edu/media/cpr.unu.edu/attachment/4844/UNU_TJ_Colombia.pdf.

Red+ Noticias. 2023. "Los tradicionales jefes guerrilleros de las Farc que han muerto." Red+ Noticias, July 6. https://redmas.com.co/Los-tradicionales-jefes-guerrilleros-de-las-Farc-que-han-muerto-t202307060001.html.

Robinson, Joseph S. 2017. *Transitional Justice and the Politics of Inscription: Memory, Space and Narrative in Northern Ireland*. 1st ed. Routledge. https://doi.org/10.4324/9781315265308.

Rodrigo Londoño. 2024. "Intervención en el Acto de comunicación de los decretos de amnistía de iure a firmantes del Acuerdo de Paz." X (formerly Twitter), February 21. https://twitter.com/TimoComunes.

Rodríguez-Raga, Juan Carlos. 2023. "El Barómetro de Las Américas Toma El Pulso de La Democracia En Colombia." In *Pulso de La Democracia En Colombia: 2023*. Barómetro de Las Américas. https://www.vanderbilt.edu/lapop/colombia/ABCOL2023-Pulso-de-la-democracia-final-20240403.pdf.

Rojas, Gabriel. 2025. "Primeras sentencias restaurativas por crímenes atroces: la justicia transicional colombiana en acción - Agenda Estado de Derecho."

Región Andina. *Agenda Estado de Derecho*, November 6. https://agendaestadodederecho.com/primeras-sentencias-restaurativas-por-crimenes-atroces/.
Romero-Prieto, Julio Enrique, and Adolfo Meisel-Roca. 2019. "Análisis Demográfico de La Violencia En Colombia." *Cuadernos de Historia Económica; No. 50.*
Sala de Reconocimiento de Verdad y Responsabilidad. 2018. *Criterios y Metodología de Priorización de Casos y Situaciones.* Jurisdicción Especial para la Paz. https://www.jep.gov.co/documents/criteriosymetodologiadepriorizacion.pdf.
Sánchez, Nelson Camilo, Leigh A. Payne, Gabriel Pereira, Laura Bernal, Daniel Marín, and Miguel Barboza. 2018. *Cuentas Claras: El Papel de la Comisión de la Verdad en la Develación de la Responsabilidad de Empresas en el Conflicto Armado Colombiano.* 1st ed. Dejusticia Series. Centro de Estudios de Derecho, Justicia y Sociedad.
Santos, Juan Manuel. 2019. *La Batalla Por La Paz.* Grupo Planeta - Colombia.
Santos, Francisco. 2025. "Teníamos razón." Semana.com Últimas Noticias de Colombia y el Mundo, September 20. https://www.semana.com/opinion/articulo/teniamos-razon/202535/.
Section of Acknowledgement of Responsibility and Truth. 2025a. *Sentence TP-SeRVR-RC-ST-001–2025.* https://relatoria.jep.gov.co//documentos/providencias/4/2/Sentencia_TP-SeRVR-RC-ST-001-2025_16-septiembre-2025.pdf.
Section of Acknowledgement of Responsibility and Truth. 2025b. *Sentence TP-SeRVR-RC-ST-002.*
Semana. 2018. "El avispero que alborotó la JEP con el caso Santrich." Semana.com Últimas Noticias de Colombia y el Mundo, May 17. https://www.semana.com/caso-santrich-la-jep-levanto-un-avispero-con-suspension-de-extradicion/567484/.
Semana. 2019a. "La vigilia en París por la JEP." Semana.com Últimas Noticias de Colombia y el Mundo, March 9. https://www.semana.com/la-protesta-en-paris-por-la-posible-objecion-a-la-jep/604961/.
Semana. 2019b. "#YoDefiendoLaJEP: El mensaje que envían 30 líderes colombianos a Duque." Semana.com Últimas Noticias de Colombia y el Mundo, February 16. https://www.semana.com/yodefiendolajep-el-mensaje-que-envian-30-lideres-colombianos-a-duque/601741/.
Semana. 2020a. "Cero y van tres: un nuevo intento por modificar la JEP." Semana.com Últimas Noticias de Colombia y el Mundo, June 1. https://www.semana.com/cero-y-van-tres-un-nuevo-intento-por-modificar-la-jep/675534/.
Semana. 2020b. "JEP recibe millonario guiño de Europa." Semana.com Últimas Noticias de Colombia y el Mundo, July 28. https://www.semana.com/jep-recibe-millonario-guino-de-europa/689713/.

Semana. 2021a. "'No es magistrado sino politiquero que aumenta la ilegitimidad de la JEP': Uribe critica a Eduardo Cifuentes." Semana.com Últimas Noticias de Colombia y el Mundo, August 30. https://www.semana.com/nacion/articulo/no-es-magistrado-sino-politiquero-que-aumenta-la-ilegitimidad-de-la-jep-uribe-critica-a-eduardo-cifuentes/202145/.

Semana. 2021b. "'Quizás, quizás' y otros sarcasmos y cinismos de Santrich." Semana.com Últimas Noticias de Colombia y el Mundo, May 18. https://www.semana.com/nacion/articulo/quizas-quizas-y-otros-sarcasmos-y-cinismos-de-santrich/202118/.

Semana. 2023a. "Expresidente Uribe revela denuncia en la que le aseguran que la magistrada de la JEP Caterina Heyck está 'obsesionada' con él." Semana.com Últimas Noticias de Colombia y el Mundo, November 19. https://www.semana.com/politica/articulo/expresidente-uribe-revela-denuncia-en-la-que-le-aseguran-que-la-magistrada-de-la-jep-caterina-heyck-esta-obsesionada-con-el/202334/.

Semana. 2023b. "Gobernadora del Valle cumplirá arresto desde este viernes y lanza duro dardo a la JEP: 'Criminales son nombrados gestores de paz.'" Semana.com Últimas Noticias de Colombia y el Mundo, December 28. https://www.semana.com/nacion/cali/articulo/gobernadora-del-valle-cumplira-arresto-desde-este-viernes-y-lanza-duro-dardo-a-la-jep-criminales-son-nombrados-gestores-de-paz/202350/.

Semana. 2023c. "Por insultar a la víctimas y llamar 'guerrilleros' a los magistrados, la JEP pide investigar penal y disciplinariamente al alcalde de Aguachica (Cesar)." Semana.com Últimas Noticias de Colombia y el Mundo, May 31. https://www.semana.com/nacion/articulo/por-insultar-a-la-victimas-y-llamar-guerrilleros-a-los-magistrados-la-jep-pide-investigar-penal-y-disciplinariamente-al-alcalde-de-aguachica-cesar/202329/.

Semana. 2024a. "Atención | JEP le responde al Secretariado de las Farc. De renunciar a comparecer perderán todos los beneficios y enfrentarán la justicia ordinaria." Semana.com Últimas Noticias de Colombia y el Mundo, February 7. https://www.semana.com/nacion/articulo/atencion-jep-le-responde-al-secretariado-de-las-farc-de-renunciar-a-comparecer-perderan-todos-los-beneficios-y-enfrentaran-la-justicia-ordinaria/202418/.

Semana. 2024b. "'Completa falsedad': magistrado Roberto Vidal les responde a excomandantes de las Farc y recuerda los 60 años de cárcel que purgarán si la JEP no les gusta." Semana.com Últimas Noticias de Colombia y el Mundo, February 27. https://www.semana.com/semana-tv/vicky-en-semana/articulo/completa-falsedad-magistrado-roberto-vidal-les-responde-a-excomandantes-de-las-farc-y-recuerda-los-60-anos-de-carcel-que-purgaran-si-la-jep-no-les-gusta/202429/.

Shany, Yuval. 2014. *Assessing the Effectiveness of International Courts*. Oxford University Press. https://doi.org/10.1093/acprof:oso/9780199643295.001.0001.

Shenk, J. L. 2022. "Democratization from below: Citizen-Activated Participatory Democracy in Colombia's Extractive Industries." PhD Thesis, University of Oxford.

Stacey, Diego. 2025. "La justicia transicional de Colombia conserva el apoyo de la ONU pese a las reticencias del Consejo de Seguridad." El País América Colombia, November 6. https://elpais.com/america-colombia/2025-11-06/la-justicia-transicional-de-colombia-conserva-el-apoyo-de-la-onu-pese-a-las-reticencias-del-consejo-de-seguridad.html.

Theodor Meron. 2003. "ICTY Oral History - Theodor Meron." Interview by ICTY Oral History Collection. October 20. https://ictyoralhistory.sensecentar.org/theodor-meron-interview.

Torres Lasso, Juan Diego. 2025. "Familiares Dividen Sus Posiciones Frente a Las Dos Sentencias de La JEP Contra 12 Militares y 7 exFarc." *El Tiempo*, September 20. https://web.archive.org/web/20251009202109/https://www.eltiempo.com/justicia/jep-colombia/familiares-dividen-sus-posiciones-frente-a-las-dos-sentencias-de-la-jep-contra-12-militares-y-7-exfarc-3492586.

Truth Commision of Colombia. 2022. *Hallazgos y recomendaciones: de la Comisión de la Verdad de Colombia*. Primera edición. Hay futuro si hay verdad, Tomo 2,3. Comisión de la Verdad.

Truth Commission of Colombia. 2022a. "Cifras de la Comisión de la Verdad presentadas junto con el Informe Final." June 11. https://web.comisiondelaverdad.co/actualidad/noticias/principales-cifras-comision-de-la-verdad-informe-final.

Truth Commission of Colombia. 2022b. *No matarás: relato histórico del conflicto armado interno en Colombia*. Primera edición. Hay futuro si hay verdad, Tomo 3,3. Comisión de la Verdad.

UN Verification Mission and JEP. 2022. "La JEP y la Misión de la ONU firman protocolo que activa el Mecanismo de Monitoreo y Verificación de las Sanciones Propias." August 16. https://www.jep.gov.co:443/Sala-de-Prensa/Paginas/La-JEP-y-la-Misi%C3%B3n-de-la-ONU-firman-protocolo-que-activa-el-Mecanismo-de-Monitoreo-y-Verificaci%C3%B3n-de-las-Sanciones-Propias-.aspx.

Unidad para la atención y reparación de las víctimas. 2023. "Registro Único de Víctimas (RUV)." Registro Único de Víctimas, February 28. https://www.unidadvictimas.gov.co/es/registro-unico-de-victimas-ruv/37394.

United Nations. 2025. "Colombia: El Consejo de Seguridad reduce el mandato de la Misión de la ONU en ese país | Noticias ONU." Paz y Seguridad, October 31. https://news.un.org/es/story/2025/10/1540672.

Unity for the Search of People Deemed as Missing. 2025. "Portal de Datos de la UBPD." May 15. https://datos.unidadbusqueda.gov.co/.

Uprimny, Rodrigo. 2018. "¿Cuál estructura para la JEP?" *Dejusticia*, January 21. https://www.dejusticia.org/column/cual-estructura-para-la-jep/.

Uprimny Yepes, Rodrigo, Maria Paula Saffón Sanin, Catalina Botero Marino, and Esteban Restrepo Saldarriaga. 2006. *¿Justicia Transicional Sin Transición? Verdad, Justicia y Reparación Para Colombia*. Dejusticia. https://www.dejusticia.org/wp-content/uploads/2017/04/fi_name_recurso_201.pdf.

Valencia, Paula Andrea, and Mateo Merchán Duque. 2025. "Las sentencias de la JEP ya están, ¿pero se pueden cumplir?" *La Silla Vacía*, October 16. https://www.lasillavacia.com/red-de-expertos/red-de-la-paz/las-sentencias-de-la-jep-ya-estan-pero-se-pueden-cumplir/.

Valencia Valencia, Paula Andrea, and Pedro Francés-Gómez. 2018. "Legitimidad de la Jurisdicción Especial para la Paz." *Revista de Paz y Conflictos* 11 (1): 105–33. https://doi.org/10.30827/revpaz.v11i1.6027.

Van Hoeven, Juliana. 2016. *Counter-Terrorism Measures and International Humanitarian Law: A Case Study of the "Troubles" in Northern Ireland*.

Villar Borda, Leopoldo. 2020. "El 'golpe de opinión' que decepcionó a Colombia." El Tiempo, June 12. https://www.eltiempo.com/colombia/otras-ciudades/dictadura-de-rojas-pinilla-golpe-de-opinion-que-decepciono-a-colombia-506522.

Voeten, Erik. 2013. "Public Opinion and the Legitimacy of International Courts." *Theoretical Inquiries in Law* (Tel Aviv) 14 (2): 411–36. https://doi.org/10.1515/til-2013-021.

Weber, Max. 2019. *Economy and Society: A New Translation*. With Keith Tribe. Ebook Central. Harvard University Press. https://ezproxy-prd.bodleian.ox.ac.uk/login?url=https://ebookcentral.proquest.com/lib/oxford/detail.action?docID=5715885.

Yesid Reyes. 2024. "Los reclamos de las extintas FARC-EP a la JEP." Text. ELESPECTADOR.COM, February 13. https://www.elespectador.com/opinion/columnistas/yesid-reyes-alvarado/los-reclamos-de-las-extintas-farc-ep-a-la-jep/.

Zartman, I William. 2001. "The Timing of Peace Initiatives: Hurting Stalemates and Ripe Moments[1]." *Global Review of Ethnopolitics* 1 (1): 8–18. https://doi.org/10.1080/14718800108405087.

Zuluaga Afanador, Nicolás. 2021. *El Cumplimiento Colectivo Del Deber de Reparación En La Jurisdicción Especial Para La Paz Desafíos y Aprendizajes Para Agilizar El Procesamiento Del Régimen de Condicionalidad*. ETJN Working Papers Series. https://repository.essex.ac.uk/31780/1/ETJN_DT3_Cumplimiento%20colectivo_new_logo.pdf.

Zulver, Julia. 2022. *High-Risk Feminism in Colombia: Women's Mobilization in Violent Contexts*. Rutgers University Press.

GPSR Compliance
The European Union's (EU) General Product Safety Regulation (GPSR) is a set of rules that requires consumer products to be safe and our obligations to ensure this.

If you have any concerns about our products, you can contact us on

ProductSafety@springernature.com

In case Publisher is established outside the EU, the EU authorized representative is:

Springer Nature Customer Service Center GmbH
Europaplatz 3
69115 Heidelberg, Germany

www.ingramcontent.com/pod-product-compliance
Ingram Content Group UK Ltd.
Pitfield, Milton Keynes, MK11 3LW, UK
UKHW020753220926
475829UK00004BA/90
* 9 7 8 3 0 3 2 2 1 9 1 1 4 *